LIFE, LOVE, AND LESSONS IN THE SKY

A Flight Attendant's Inspiring Journey

Lia Ocampo

DEDICATION

For those who *DREAM*.
For those who *LOVE*.
and
For those who *INSPIRE*.

CONTENTS

PREFACE

For ten unforgettable years, the sky was my second home. With every takeoff and landing, I discovered that this career was far more than a job—it was a calling. Each flight became a vibrant tapestry woven with adventure, challenge, and connection. I poured my passion into every aisle and cabin, transforming ordinary journeys into extraordinary moments.

My time in aviation was a symphony of experiences. I met travelers whose stories shimmered with inspiration, navigated turbulence and emergencies, braved winter storms, and endured long delays that tested patience. There were late nights filled with laughter that made stress dissolve, and mornings where lighthearted banter with passengers turned cramped cabins into spaces of joy. I encountered both kindness and rudeness, moments of ease and moments of chaos. Yet through it all, I discovered resilience, empathy, and the remarkable ways lives intersect at 35,000 feet.

These memories—shaped by passengers, colleagues, and my own moments of triumph and failure—inspired me to write this book. Each story is a treasure, and each lesson a reflection of what it means to be human, even in the most unexpected places. Within these pages, you'll find glimpses of life behind the curtain of aviation, as well as reflections on the spirit that unites us when we're suspended between earth and sky.

Let this book serve as both an invitation and a confession: an invitation to witness the hidden dramas and quiet acts of grace above the clouds, and a confession of my own awe at the beauty, complexity, and wonder of this profession. Whether you're a fellow traveler, a dreamer with eyes lifted to the sky, or someone searching for meaning in life's fleeting moments, I welcome you to step beyond the boarding gate.

Here, every flight becomes more than just a journey, and every mile carries the promise of inspiration. May you find in these stories courage for your challenges, compassion for fleeting encounters, and wonder in the everyday. Above all, I encourage you to dream boldly, love deeply, and live a life that inspires others.

♥

Flying starts with a dream.

- Flying Author Lia

INTRODUCTION

Above the clouds, life takes on a different perspective. The world below — bustling, noisy, and unpredictable — feels distant, almost like a memory. From the narrow aisles of an airplane to the quiet moments in layover hotels, I've witnessed life in all its complexity: joy and sorrow, humor and humility, triumph and tragedy. As a flight attendant, I've had the privilege of touching countless lives, sharing fleeting connections with passengers, mentoring colleagues, and finding lessons in moments both ordinary and extraordinary.

Life, Love, and Lessons in the Sky: A Flight Attendant's Inspiring Journey is more than a memoir — it is a tapestry of stories drawn from my years in the air, each one reflecting resilience, compassion, and human connection. Through turbulence and smooth skies, I've learned that life, much like flying, is unpredictable. Plans shift, challenges appear unannounced, and every goodbye carries the possibility of finality. And yet, it is in these very moments of uncertainty that the most meaningful lessons emerge.

This book is my invitation to you: to soar alongside me as I share the highs and lows, the laughter and tears, the quiet victories and life-changing encounters that have shaped my journey. From the heartwarming moments of connecting with passengers, to the trials of mentorship, to lessons in patience, grace, and love, each chapter offers a glimpse into the lessons the sky has taught me — and continues to teach.

Whether you are drawn to stories of resilience, searching for inspiration, or simply curious about life behind the cabin doors, I hope these pages remind you that beauty and meaning can be found in every flight, every interaction, and every moment we have. Life is not always smooth, but when we navigate it with love, courage, and a willingness to learn, every journey becomes extraordinary.

Welcome aboard.

CONGRATULATIONS, YOU'RE HIRED!

I arrived in New York in 2012 with two suitcases, a heart full of hope, and a dream bigger than the city skyline. I was an immigrant from the Philippines, stepping onto American soil with equal parts fear and determination. I didn't know what the future held, but I was certain of one thing: I wanted to work with the United Nations. The U.N. had always symbolized peace, dignity, and equality for me. If I could be part of that mission, I believed my journey across the ocean would be worth every sacrifice.

New York, however, is a city that tests your resolve. The skyscrapers rise like fortresses, the subway roars like a restless beast, and the streets teem with people chasing their own ambitions. I felt both lost and energized, as if the city were asking me to prove myself worthy of my dreams.

When I found an opening at the United Nations Women, my heart skipped. This was my chance. I submitted my application, poured all my hopes into that single click, and waited. A few weeks later, I was invited to a personal interview. The message felt like a divine sign. I prepared with intensity, spending days reading everything I could about the organization's initiatives, memorizing mission statements, and rehearsing responses in front of my mirror. By the time the day arrived, I believed I was ready.

The interview itself was both a blur and a sharp memory. I remember the polished floors, the professional tone, the seriousness in the air. I answered each question with confidence, convinced I had left a good impression. When I walked out of the building, I felt victorious. I believed the position was mine.

But a few days later, an email arrived in my inbox. I opened it eagerly, only to find the words I dreaded: *We regret to inform you...*

The disappointment sank deep. My chest tightened, and I remember staring at the screen, rereading the words as if repetition could change them. For a moment, I felt foolish for even trying. Was I dreaming too big? Had I misunderstood my place in this vast, competitive world?

But life has a way of teaching you resilience. After a day of sadness, I made a choice. If the U.N. wasn't ready for me, then I would keep moving forward. A rejection was not an ending. It was a redirection.

Over the following year, I worked a string of short jobs that were both humbling and enlightening. I became a recruiter at a nonprofit, a personal shopper at Macy's, and a customer service representative at NYC Consumer Affairs. I even dabbled in editing and human resources at a K-pop company. Each role tested me in different ways. Some were challenging, others were mundane, but all brought lessons.

I learned patience from dealing with demanding customers. I learned empathy from listening to people's stories. I learned discipline   from   balancing   long   shifts   with   personal responsibilities. Yet despite these lessons, something remained missing. My days were full, but not fulfilling. At night, lying in bed, I felt restless. My heart whispered that I was not where I was meant to be.

During these quiet hours, I remembered my childhood dream. Long before the United Nations had entered my imagination, I had looked up at the sky and wished to become a flight attendant. I wanted to travel the world, meet people from different cultures, and live a life of adventure. That dream had been buried beneath practicality, but now it resurfaced with urgency.

I began researching airlines, scouring websites for opportunities. That's when I found that Endeavor Air, a wholly-owned subsidiary of Delta Air Lines, was hiring. My pulse quickened. This could be the door I had been waiting for. I completed the online application with care, double-checking every detail, and sent it off with a silent prayer.

Not long after, an email arrived inviting me to an in-person screening and interview in Arlington, Virginia. Excitement coursed through me. I felt a sense of destiny.

The night before the event, I traveled to Virginia and stayed at the hotel where the hiring event was held. I carefully laid out my outfit: a sharp business suit, polished shoes, and subtle makeup. I wanted to look the part, to embody the confidence and professionalism of a flight attendant. Sleep was restless that night, my mind rehearsing scenarios, my heart leaping between hope and fear.

When morning came, I arrived early. The room buzzed with other candidates, each dressed impeccably, each carrying the same dream. Registration went smoothly, and I noticed the committee members exchanging approving glances at my presentation. Their compliments bolstered my confidence, but I knew the real test lay ahead.

One of the first challenges was the arm-reach test, a requirement to ensure that flight attendants could access safety equipment during emergencies. Candidates lined up nervously, stretching to touch the mark on the wall. When my turn came, doubt flickered in me. What if I couldn't reach it?

At that moment, I heard a voice—Maryann, one of the recruiters, smiling warmly and cheering me on. "You can do it!" she said. Her encouragement pierced through my fear. With renewed determination, I reached up, touched the mark, and passed. Relief washed over me, mingled with gratitude for her support.

The rest of the day unfolded with interviews, a customer service presentation, and reading the customer service announcement. I gave it everything I had, drawing on my past experiences in customer service and recruitment. I showed them my enthusiasm, my adaptability, and my genuine love for people. By the time I left, I felt cautiously optimistic.

Then came the waiting. Days stretched into weeks. Every time I checked my email, my heart raced. And then, one morning, it was there: an email with the subject line *Congratulations!*

Tears blurred my vision as I read the message. I had been hired. The word felt like music, the sweetest affirmation I had ever received. I had left the Philippines with a dream, faced rejection and uncertainty, but now I was stepping into my calling.

Training was rigorous. We learned emergency equipment and protocols, medical and safety procedures, security, federal regulations, dangerous goods, crew resource management, and the delicate art of customer service at 35,000 feet. There were moments I felt overwhelmed, but my determination never wavered. I was finally living the life I had imagined.

When I stepped onto the aircraft for my first official flight, dressed in my crisp uniform, wings pinned proudly to my chest, I felt a rush of pride. The hum of the engines, the chatter of passengers, the organized chaos of boarding — all of it filled me with joy. This was where I belonged.

Being a flight attendant was more than just a job. It was an adventure. Each flight carried new faces, new stories, new horizons. I traveled to places I had only dreamed of, meeting people from every corner of the world. My rejection from U.N. Women no longer felt like a failure. It was a blessing in disguise. If I had been accepted, I might never have discovered the path that truly fulfilled me.

Three years later, a new opportunity arose. I was invited to become a flight attendant recruiter. The irony wasn't lost on me — I had once been the nervous candidate, now I was the one welcoming others, encouraging them as Maryann had encouraged me.

As a recruiter, I understood the hope and fear in each applicant's eyes. I remembered the weight of waiting for that one word — *Congratulations*. Helping others reach that moment became a mission close to my heart. For a year, I guided candidates, offered advice, and celebrated their successes. Each time someone was hired, I felt a spark of joy, knowing I had played a small role in changing their lives.

Looking back, my journey has been filled with hope, resilience, setbacks, and triumphs. I learned that rejection is not the end, but a redirection. Every job I took before becoming a flight attendant added to my skill set, shaping me into a stronger candidate. Preparation, perseverance, and a willingness to embrace support made all the difference.

To anyone dreaming of a career in the sky, here are lessons I carry with me:

- **Resilience in the face of rejection.** Don't let one "no" end your journey. Sometimes rejection is simply a detour to something better.

- **Continuous learning.** Every experience, no matter how small, can build your character and skills.

- **Preparation matters.** Study, practice, and present yourself with confidence. Effort shines through.

- **Support counts.** Encouragement from others can lift you when you falter. Be that voice for someone else, too.

- **Pursue your passion.** Don't settle for a career that doesn't spark joy. Keep searching until you find what lights your spirit.

- **Be adaptable.** Flight schedules change, life changes, but flexibility keeps you moving forward.

- **Stay enthusiastic.** Genuine care and energy distinguish you in any profession.

Today, when I reflect on my journey from the Philippines to New York, from rejection letters to hiring emails, from a nervous applicant to a confident recruiter, I see a story of persistence and faith. My path didn't unfold the way I first envisioned, but it unfolded exactly as it needed to.

For anyone chasing a dream—whether it's in the skies or on the ground—remember this: your journey may twist and turn, but each step carries you closer to where you belong. Rejection isn't failure; it's preparation. And when the time is right, the email will arrive, the call will come, and the words you've been waiting for will finally appear.

Congratulations. You're hired!

FINDING DANIEL

Sharing our time is giving the one thing we can never regain. When we offer it freely, it transforms the ordinary into something extraordinary. It is not just about what we sacrifice, but about what we create. A few moments of comfort can ease a burden. A quiet word can become a safe harbor in the storm. And sometimes, one act of kindness grows into a memory that stays alive long after the moment has passed.

I was reminded of this truth during a flight from Bangor, Maine, to LaGuardia Airport. While greeting passengers, I noticed a woman who immediately stood out to me. Her name was Hannah. She looked distracted, clutching her phone tightly, her eyes red and tired as if she had been crying. There was a kind of urgency in her silence, a weight that seemed to press down on her shoulders. Something in me told me she was carrying more than just a suitcase.

I decided to give her some space, sensing she needed quiet. I gently asked the passenger sitting next to her if she wouldn't mind moving to an open row, and she agreed. Before she left, she whispered to me what Hannah was going through. Her son, Daniel, had been reported missing.

Daniel was in his thirties, an English teacher working in South Korea, and someone with special needs. His employment at the school has ended, and his family has arranged for his return to the United States. But somewhere along the way, plans shifted. After missing a connection, Daniel seemed to vanish. His family hadn't heard from him for a day. He had no U.S. phone number, which only increased their fears. Daniel was supposed to arrive home in Maine the night before, but he never showed up.

Hannah had been desperate enough to purchase a last-minute ticket to New York, determined to go to JFK Airport herself to search for him. She confided in me that she was unfamiliar with JFK, that it had been years since she'd traveled there, and she felt terrified at the thought of trying to navigate its sprawling, chaotic terminals alone.

I listened to her quietly, my heart aching as I imagined her fear. It was my last day of a four-day trip, and my original plan was to catch a flight to Jacksonville, Florida, and head home. But when I looked at Hannah's face, I knew my plans could wait. I couldn't let her go through this journey alone. Sometimes we don't need to think twice about doing the right thing. So, I decided to stay with her and help search for Daniel.

We boarded the Golden Touch bus from LaGuardia to JFK, a shuttle I had taken countless times, but this time felt different. The ride was filled with uncertainty. Hannah held her phone like a lifeline, waiting for news. Halfway through the trip, a message finally came. Her daughter had heard from Daniel. He had borrowed a Delta phone and said he was safe. He would be on the 10:30 PM flight.

For a moment, relief flooded Hannah's face. Her shoulders relaxed, and her breathing grew steadier. Still, I could sense the nervous energy that lingered. Words were one thing. Seeing Daniel in person would be the real assurance.

When we arrived at Terminal 4, we began our search. Our first stop was gate B18, where his flight had been scheduled. Daniel wasn't there. We walked to B55, hoping he might be waiting there instead. Nothing. Each waiting area echoed with travelers heading in every direction, but none of the faces matched the one Hannah longed to see.

We decided to check Terminal 2, where Daniel's flight was supposed to depart later that night. The two of us moved quickly, weaving through crowds, scanning every corner. I kept encouraging Hannah, reminding her that we were getting closer. Just as we were about to page Daniel, another message came through. He was at B55 in Terminal 4.

Back we went. Despite the exhaustion settling into her steps, Hannah's pace quickened. Her eyes darted through the crowd until suddenly, they locked on a familiar silhouette. She gasped, rushed forward, and in an instant, mother and son were wrapped in each other's arms. The hug was long, desperate, and overflowing with relief.

I stood back for a moment, letting them have the reunion they had both been waiting for. Wanting Hannah to have a keepsake of this moment, I quickly snapped a photo. For them, that picture would be more than just an image. It would be proof that hope had carried them through.

Daniel looked drained, confused, and a little anxious as he explained what had happened. Missing the flight, being alone, and not having a U.S. phone number had left him feeling lost.

Hannah listened patiently, her eyes full of compassion. She reassured him with gentle words, her voice steady now that she had him in her arms.

I contacted crew scheduling to let the captain know about Hannah and Daniel's flight to Portland, Maine. I asked that they receive special attention on board, so their final stretch home would be as smooth as possible. Later, Hannah told me Daniel had been pleasantly surprised by how kind the pilot was, a small act of care that meant the world after such harrowing days.

In the days that followed, Hannah and I stayed in touch. She sent me several messages, but one in particular stays etched in my heart.

"My son is doing better. It was a long, hard time getting him to accept help and be diagnosed. It will be a long road before he can be independent again, but I am holding together. Sometimes I fall apart for a little while, then I pick up the pieces. I think of you often. Your incredible kindness gives me hope."

Reading her words, I felt a quiet sense of fulfillment. My career often demands long hours and constant travel. It can be exhausting. Yet moments like this remind me why I keep going. The skies are not just highways between cities; they are meeting places for stories, intersections where strangers can become allies, and where compassion can shine brightest.

Looking back, I realize how extraordinary that day was. I could have gone home to rest, but instead, I chose to walk alongside Hannah in her search. It cost me time, but what I received was immeasurable: the honor of witnessing a mother's love, the joy of seeing Daniel safely reunited with his family, and the reminder that kindness is never wasted.

Our paths crossed by chance, but the bond we formed that day was real. The story of finding Daniel is not only about one missing son, but about hope, resilience, and the power of human connection. It is a story that will stay with me for the rest of my life.

A MILESTONE

Martha sat by the window, her silver-streaked hair catching the light as the morning sun filtered through the cabin. Her face, softly lined with years of laughter and love, carried the unmistakable warmth of a grandmother. On her lap rested a well-worn handbag, the kind that seemed to have carried decades of memories. Her eyes, however, sparkled with the brightness of a child on Christmas morning.

She was in her seventies, celebrating her birthday with her friend, and for the very first time in her life, she was flying. Ahead of her waited New York City and her son, whom she hadn't seen in years.

From the very beginning, her excitement was contagious. She leaned close to the window as the engines roared, gripping her friend's hand as the aircraft lifted into the clouds. The sunlight shimmered across the wings, casting golden reflections on her face. Even the gentle tilt of the plane as we banked eastward seemed to thrill her. For seasoned travelers, these were ordinary details. For Martha, each one was magic, each moment a memory waiting to be made.

I couldn't help but notice her delight. It radiated across the cabin, drawing me toward her row. When I paused to check in, she greeted me with a wide, easy smile. That's when she revealed it was her first time flying. I asked why, and she chuckled, the kind of laugh that carried both humor and tenderness. "I was busy raising three boys," she said. "I never had the chance. But now? Now is the perfect time to celebrate with my son."

Her words struck me deeply. Decades of motherhood had kept her grounded, her own dreams quietly waiting. And here she was, finally stepping into the sky, proof that some journeys may be delayed but never denied.

The crew wanted her milestone to feel unforgettable. We gave her a birthday card, a flight attendant wing, a glass of wine, and even a cockpit tour. Martha received every gesture with gratitude and delight. Her wit and gentle charm made her the center of attention. I remember wishing we had a birthday cake for her. She deserved one. Yet even without it, her laughter and glowing presence made the entire flight feel like a celebration.

At 35,000 feet, I realized something important: milestones aren't always about grand achievements. Sometimes, they're about courage, the courage to embrace something new, no matter when it happens. Martha's first flight wasn't just her victory. It became a celebration shared by her friend, our crew, and every passenger who glimpsed her joy.

As we began our descent into New York, Martha pressed closer to the window, her wide eyes taking in the glittering skyline. The city stretched across the horizon, bright and vast, no longer a dream but a destination within her grasp. When the doors opened, her friend gently took her arm, steadying her steps as they walked down the jet bridge together. I watched them disappear into the crowd, two friends stepping into possibility, their faces lit with anticipation.

For Martha, each step was more than a movement. It was a declaration that life still held first, that age was no barrier, and that it is never too late for adventure. She reminded me that the milestones worth remembering aren't measured in years, but in the courage to say *yes* to the unknown.

WHO TWEETED MY CHOCOLATES?

T he night of January 11, 2020, is etched in my memory. We were bound for Ottawa, Canada, when the weather turned against us, forcing the small regional jet I was working on to divert unexpectedly to Burlington, Vermont. The storm was relentless, the kind that makes the world outside vanish into a blur of snow and gray.

As the sole flight attendant, I felt the weight of responsibility pressing heavily on my shoulders. The flight stretched late into the night, then bled into the following day. Fatigue was etched on every face, and yet, to my surprise, the passengers were patient, kind, and understanding. Nobody enjoys delays, diversions, or cancellations, but this group met the chaos with grace. Their calm gave me the strength to keep going.

Still, I wanted to do something more—something that might lighten the mood and remind them that they were cared for. The next morning, during a short break, I slipped away and bought a big bag of chocolates. They weren't fancy, just simple sweets, but as I handed them out row by row, the cabin began to change. Smiles appeared, shoulders eased, and the air shifted from weary silence to soft laughter. What began as an impulsive gesture of gratitude quickly became a shared moment of comfort.

One passenger, Donna, stood out. She had kind eyes and an open smile, the kind of person who makes you feel seen even in passing. As I offered her the chocolates, she asked if she could take a photo and share the story. I didn't think much of it at the time. To me, it was just a small act of kindness.

But Donna's tweet carried the story far beyond our little plane in Vermont:

"We are home and safe. Thank you, Lia. You made a crappy situation much better. I hope Delta knows what a wonderful employee you are."

And another, with my photo:

"This is our flight attendant, Lia, who deserves recognition. After DL 5477 was diverted from Ottawa, Ontario, to Burlington, Vermont last night, she has saved the flight! She personally bought us chocolates today. Now that is customer service!"

I read her words later with a lump in my throat. What I had thought of as something small had traveled further than I ever imagined.

That day reminded me that when you care about your work, you look for ways to rise to challenges, even when the circumstances are out of your control. Small gestures can ripple outward, touching not only those directly involved but also strangers who hear the story.

Not every act of kindness will be noticed or celebrated, and sometimes that can sting. But the true reward lies in the act itself — the quiet joy of knowing you tried to ease someone else's burden. For me, those chocolates will always be a reminder that compassion, no matter how simple, has the power to turn a stormy night into a story of gratitude.

NEVER QUIT

The words "Never Quit" sound simple, but they hold a depth that can steady a weary heart. Resilience isn't always found in extraordinary victories. More often, it shows up quietly, in the determined footsteps of those who refuse to give in to life's difficulties.

This reminds me of an older traveler I once met. She was traveling alone, and I admired that. I've always admired older travelers who journey alone. They move with a mix of courage and determination that humbles me, proof that the human spirit can push forward even as the body slows. It was during one of my early morning flights from Syracuse, New York, to JFK that I met her, and she beautifully embodied that truth.

She boarded carefully, her movements deliberate, and I was told she had vision difficulties and would need extra assistance. Yet there was no hesitation in her step. She carried herself with quiet strength, offering a polite smile and a soft word of thanks each time someone reached out to help. Something about her presence drew me in—her steadiness, her calm gratitude, or maybe just the resilience etched in the way she held herself.

Throughout the flight, I kept an eye on her. When I finally had a chance to sit beside her, she spoke in the sweetest, most delicate voice, explaining that she traveled regularly to New

York City for therapy sessions. I listened, admiring her courage, though my heart ached at the thought of her doing this alone. I really wished she had someone beside her to ease the burden. But life doesn't always provide companions, and sometimes strength means walking the most challenging roads by yourself.

That afternoon, I was surprised to see her again—this time boarding the return flight from JFK back to Syracuse. Her therapy session was done for the day, and I was grateful to care for her once more. This time, she had a gift for me.

As we settled into the air, she reached into her small bag and handed me a handmade bracelet. Its woven threads carried a simple design, one that spelled out the words, "Never Quit." With a smile, she explained that she volunteers at a hospital, crafting these bracelets for patients as small tokens of hope. Then, leaning closer, she whispered, "This is for you, to thank you for caring for me."

I hugged her tightly, touched more deeply than words could express. The bracelet was light, but its meaning was heavy, filled with grace and resilience. In that moment, we were no longer just a flight attendant and a passenger. We were two travelers connected by courage, sharing a silent promise to keep moving forward no matter what.

As she prepared to deplane, I watched her careful steps down the aisle. She didn't say much, but she didn't need to. Her very presence reminded me that bravery often wears an ordinary face. Since that day, I've worn her bracelet as a reminder to keep showing up, to keep going, and to never quit—even when life feels heavy.

Some gifts don't fade with time. They keep whispering to you long after the moment has passed. Hers was one of them.

A PRAYER

The gentle hum of airplane engines has witnessed countless prayers. In the space between departure and arrival, something sacred emerges among strangers suspended thousands of feet above the earth. I've learned to watch for these quiet moments of faith, but one encounter showed me their true power.

I first noticed Maria as we boarded the evening flight from Maryland to New York. She moved with quiet grace down the aisle, her hair pulled back simply, her weathered hands clutching a worn purse. When she smiled at me with a genuine, warm greeting, I felt an immediate sense of peace radiating from her presence.

Three rows in front of me, Maria's hands moved in a familiar rhythm over smooth rosary beads. Her lips formed silent words I couldn't hear but somehow felt. As our plane lifted into the darkening sky, her quiet devotion anchored the cabin's energy. Throughout the journey, her prayers created a rhythm as steady as the engines. During turbulence when others gripped armrests nervously, Maria's hands continued their gentle dance across the beads, her expression serene. Her faith transformed our cramped cabin into a sacred space, a chapel at 35,000 feet where vulnerability became courage.

I found myself checking on her periodically, not from concern but from wonder. Here was someone who had turned ordinary air travel into a pilgrimage, each bead marking a step deeper into communion with the divine. Her quiet confidence was contagious. The longer I watched her pray, the more my own anxieties settled into something resembling peace.

When we began our descent into JFK Airport, Maria carefully tucked her rosary away. As we waited to deplane, she tapped my shoulder gently and held out a small card depicting Our Lady of Guadalupe, the Virgin's serene face surrounded by golden rays.

"Para usted," she said softly, pressing the card into my palm. "I will pray for you." Her English carried Spanish's musical cadence, and her eyes held warmth that crosses all language barriers.

The card was smooth from handling, edges worn, suggesting it was one of many she carried for moments like this. As I thanked her, she nodded and patted my hand with the gesture of a grandmother blessing a grandchild.

That small piece of cardstock carried more weight than any souvenir I'd ever received. It represented something profound about human connection—how a stranger's faith becomes a bridge across cultures and languages. In that brief exchange, Maria had transformed our shared journey from mere transportation into something sacred.

Our Lady of Guadalupe holds special significance in Mexican culture. I had visited her magnificent shrine in Mexico City with my Aunt Siony in 2016, marveling at streams of faithful carrying flowers and prayers. Standing among thousands of believers, I felt the same universal connection that Maria's simple gift now evoked.

The prayer card sits on my desk as I write this, a daily reminder of an encounter lasting mere minutes but resonating months later. It reminds me that prayer isn't merely a private conversation with the divine but a gesture creating invisible threads between souls.

In our fragmented world where strangers remain strangers, Maria's gift testifies to a different way of being. Her prayers weren't just for safe passage but for all of us suspended together, trusting our lives to physics and faith in equal measure.

There's something profoundly beautiful about these unplanned encounters with grace. They arrive when we need them most, reminding us that kindness recognizes no borders and compassion requires no common language. Maria's prayer card has become more than a souvenir. It's a call to acknowledge the sacred in ordinary moments and to see strangers as fellow travelers.

Perhaps this is prayer's true nature: not just a request for divine intervention, but an act of faith that connects us to something larger than individual concerns. In the space between takeoff and landing, between stranger and friend,

Maria showed me that grace travels at every altitude, carried in willing hearts and shared through simple gestures that transform ordinary moments into extraordinary memories.

A FLIGHT CLOSE TO MY HEART

T he plastic bag with the ICMC logo was unmistakable. As a family from the Middle East boarded our flight to Syracuse in June 2016, I immediately recognized the International Catholic Migration Commission documents each person carried, the same papers I had once helped prepare for other refugee families seeking new lives in America.

The parents held their young child close, faces showing that mix of nervousness and anticipation I knew so well. Their eyes took in everything: the flight attendants' uniforms, the seat numbers, the miracle of being on an airplane bound for their new home.

"Welcome to America," I said, approaching their seats with a smile. "Good luck in your new life." The father nodded gratefully, his wife clutching their documents tighter, and I felt the profound weight of that moment, the circle of my own journey completing itself.

Years earlier, I had spent four years working for the International Catholic Migration Commission, carefully processing the documents of asylum seekers and refugees hoping to enter the United States. Most were Vietnamese refugees fleeing turmoil in their homeland. Though I never met them in person, I often imagined the moment they would receive the news that their applications had been approved—the relief, the tears, the hope for a safer future. My work back then taught me that every file represented more than paperwork. It represented the chance to begin again.

Sitting on that flight years later, watching this family settle into their seats, I was reminded of all the unseen hands and hearts that help make such journeys possible. That moment was a quiet reminder that sometimes our behind-the-scenes work can change the course of someone's life—even if we never meet them face-to-face.

In 2012, I found myself on the other side of that experience. After serving the U.S. government for eighteen years, I was granted the opportunity to immigrate to America with my family. I remember my own nervousness during those first days, the kindness of strangers who helped me navigate my new country, and the overwhelming gratitude I felt for this second chance. I understood then, in a deeply personal way, what those families I had once helped were feeling.

Now, as I welcome immigrant families on our flights to cities like Syracuse, Buffalo, and Rochester, I see my own story reflected in their faces. The quiet determination, the protective way they hold their children, the careful attention to every instruction—I recognize it all. These passengers carry more than luggage; they carry hope, dreams, and the weight of starting over.

Each time I encounter these families, I'm reminded that we are all seekers of better opportunities for ourselves and our loved ones. The circumstances that bring us to new places may differ, but the human desire to thrive remains constant.

I think of the support I received during my own transition, the people who believed in me, and what I could contribute. That same spirit of welcome is what I try to extend to every immigrant family I meet. They are people seeking what we all want: safety, opportunity, and the chance to build a meaningful life.

These moments have taught me that immigration is about the courage to believe in tomorrow. As someone who has experienced both sides of this journey, helping others find their way to America and finding my own way here, I understand that every immigrant story is ultimately a story about hope.

As John F. Kennedy once said, "Everywhere immigrants have enriched and strengthened the fabric of American life." Each family I welcome aboard represents new threads in that enduring fabric, weaving their dreams into the larger American story that continues to unfold, one flight at a time.

♥

A GOOD HEART

Kindness is one of the most meaningful gifts anyone can receive, especially when it happens unexpectedly. It's rarely the grand gestures that linger in memory, but the quiet, ordinary ways we connect with each other. In a busy world, a simple word of appreciation can echo in the heart long after it is spoken.

Christmas has always been my favorite time of year. It's a season when people seem to soften — becoming more generous, forgiving, and open-hearted. The air feels lighter, as if kindness itself is in abundance.

One December, I was working flights in and out of Cincinnati, Ohio. The holiday rush was in full swing, and I had been working back-to-back legs without much rest. By the time we landed, I was drained — my feet sore, my smile a little tired around the edges.

As passengers began to leave the aircraft, a woman paused by my galley. She looked me in the eye and said softly, *"You have a good heart."*

Her words stopped me in my tracks. For a moment, I couldn't even respond. Had I done anything special for her? As far as I could remember, I had only done my job—served snacks and coffee, offered help where needed, smiled at passengers as I always tried to do. Yet, to her, that was enough.

That fleeting compliment stayed with me long after the flight was over. Somehow, it made the fatigue lighter and the day brighter. I realized then that what touches another person isn't always the big, deliberate act we imagine—it can be as simple as a warm smile, a patient tone, or the way we make someone feel seen.

I carry her words with me as a reminder. Compliments like hers don't just brighten a day; they ripple outward. They motivate me to offer the same—to tell someone I admire their kindness, or that they handled something gracefully, or that their smile made me smile too. Genuine praise costs nothing, but it can shift the course of a moment, a day, or even a life.

When I think of that woman in Cincinnati, I'm reminded that kindness isn't seasonal. It isn't reserved for Christmas or special occasions. It is a thread we can weave into our lives daily, no matter how tired or distracted we may feel.

Kind words nourish the soul. They affirm our humanity. And when someone tells you that you have a good heart, perhaps the greatest truth in that moment is this: it takes one to know one.

♥

A NOTE OF GRATITUDE

Positive energy quickly spreads and greatly influences others. Gratitude can be expressed in many ways. It might be conveyed with simple words or a note. Sincere gratitude doesn't require grand gestures; it can be shown in any form.

A lady handed me this note written on a napkin as she was deplaning. It says:

"Thank you for your exceptional service! Right when we boarded, I felt your positive energy. You work friendly & welcoming, and I noticed a sense of confidence & pride in your work. As a teacher, that is something I often try to impart with students. You have gone above & beyond in your service on our flight - and we thank you. You sharing your positive energy with the passengers matters . . . it helps all of us see your example and hopefully go forward in our day doing the same. "

– The Greens from Indiana

As I reflect on the heartfelt note that Mrs. Green penned on a simple napkin, I'm reminded of the profound impact that small gestures can have on our lives. Though I've long forgotten the exact moment that prompted her words of gratitude, the memory of her appreciation has stayed with me, a testament to the enduring power of kindness.

In my experience, moments like these are rare but incredibly motivating. They remind me that like-minded people tend to attract each other, drawn together by a shared sense of purpose and positivity. When we radiate warmth and kindness, it can spread far and wide, touching the lives of those around us in ways both big and small.

I'm grateful for people like Mrs. Green who see the authenticity in my actions and inspire me to be my best self. Her note was more than just a thank-you; it was a reminder that our efforts, no matter how small they may seem, can have a lasting impact on others. It's a feeling that resonates deeply within me, and one that I'm eager to pass on to others.

As I think about the ripple effect of that simple note, I'm struck by the realization that small acts of kindness can have far-reaching consequences. A kind word, a smile, or a thoughtful gesture can uplift not just the person directly involved but also those who witness or hear about it. In a world that often values grand gestures over small ones, it's easy to overlook the impact of these fleeting moments. Yet, it's precisely these moments that quietly connect us with compassion and empathy.

Each of us has the power to plant seeds of encouragement that, over time, grow into a quiet force for good. Imagine the collective change if we made it a habit to express gratitude more often and acknowledge the good in others. It doesn't require grand gestures or elaborate plans; just a willingness to be present, to see the positive, and to share it with others. By doing so, we not only improve the lives of those around us but also cultivate a sense of fulfillment and purpose within ourselves.

As I look back on that brief exchange with Mrs. Green, I'm reminded of the profound impact that small moments can have on our lives. We can be the reason someone smiles today, and we can trust that the energy we share will come back to us when we least expect it. In the end, it's not about grand gestures or monumental acts; it's about the small, everyday moments that weave together to form the fabric of our lives.

THERE IS HOPE

Hope is more than just words; it's a lifeline of encouragement, comfort, and a promise of brighter days ahead, even in the darkest moments. At its core, hope is the gentle assurance that pain is temporary and challenges can be overcome. When we share hope, we express our faith in someone's strength, the resilience of the human spirit, and the possibility of change.

As I stood at the back of the plane, watching passengers board, I noticed a woman in her mid-fifties struggling with her luggage. The worn handles seemed to dig into her hands, and her steps were slow and deliberate. I offered to help her, but she politely declined, insisting she could manage it herself. Her eyes, though, told a different story – a story of weariness and worry.

As we took off, the scent of freshly brewed coffee wafted through the cabin, and the sound of murmured conversations filled the air. I struck up a conversation with the woman, asking if she was going home. Her response was laced with a quiet confidence that was both inspiring and heartbreaking. "I have a brain tumor and am scheduled for surgery at the Mayo Clinic," she said, her voice barely above a whisper. "I recently learned about my condition, and I'm uncertain how long I'll stay."

In that moment, I felt a deep sense of empathy and compassion. I asked if she was traveling solo, and she mentioned that her brother would meet her at the hospital. I was moved to write her a note: "This trip may or may not be a good flight for you. Nevertheless, after your surgery, you'll have a new life. Welcome to your new world, one that's healthier and full of hope, resilience, and strength. We'll pray for you. Take care, and it's our pleasure to meet you. Hope to see you again." As I handed her the note, I could see the faintest glimmer of hope in her eyes, a spark that seemed to grow brighter as she read the words.

She expressed her gratitude, her voice filled with emotion, and though I couldn't erase her pain, I could offer her my attention, words of hope, and a prayer. In that moment, I felt a sense of connection, a sense of shared humanity that transcended our circumstances.

In the days that followed, her story lingered with me like a soft echo. I realized how easily we can overlook the quiet bravery of those around us. Every person we meet, whether a stranger, friend, or family member, might be carrying hidden burdens, yet inside them, there's often an incredible desire to keep moving forward. This encounter reminded me that hope isn't just something given or received; it's shared, quietly growing with every act of kindness.

Ultimately, hope is a powerful force that keeps us moving when the path ahead isn't clear. By sharing hope, we become part of someone's healing and resilience, reminding them that even in the hardest moments, there's still a reason to hold on. In doing so, we also remind ourselves that hope grows through sharing, quietly changing both the giver and the receiver. Showing hope is an act of kindness, a guiding light, and sometimes, exactly what's needed to help someone find their way through the storm.

A STAR

O ccasionally, we meet someone whose words change our perspective, someone who holds up a mirror and helps us see our own light, like a shining star.

One such moment happened as I boarded a flight to Raleigh-Durham, North Carolina. Passengers greeted me with applause since they had been waiting for me after a delayed inbound flight. Among them was a friendly passenger named Glenda, a retired nurse from Haiti traveling to her grandson's graduation. I had recently visited Haiti, so we quickly found common ground and began sharing stories. During our conversation, she noticed the scar on my left hand and said it looked like a star. I explained that it came from a past culinary mishap, and that I jokingly call it my "world map" tattooed on my skin.

Glenda smiled and affectionately called me a star. "You're sitting with a star," she said, encouraging me to embrace my scars and give myself credit for being kind, comparing my spirit to the glow of a star. Her words lingered between us, a gentle invitation to see myself in a new light. What I had always thought of as proof of my lack of cooking skills suddenly became, in her eyes, a symbol of something celestial, guiding its own story.

As we continued talking, I realized how strangers can uncover beauty in the very things we tend to overlook. Glenda's kindness transformed what I had considered a flaw into a shining feature. Her words stayed with me as the plane climbed above the clouds, reminding me that each of us carries parts of our journey, visible or hidden, waiting for someone kind enough to notice.

When someone calls you a star, that light has a way of staying with you and inspiring you to shine a little brighter. In my work, no matter how ordinary it may seem to others, there are moments like this, unexpected recognitions that leave a lasting impact.

Perhaps that is why stars have always fascinated me. Since childhood, I've loved watching the night sky, waiting for the rare gift of a shooting star. Even now, when I spot one, I make a wish, holding on to the hope that it will come true. That's how much stars mean to me.

It sometimes takes the wisdom of a stranger to remind us that we are already shining, even when we don't see our own glow. Kindness, after all, leaves a mark more enduring than any scar. Each scar, visible or invisible, carries the stories we've survived, the lessons we've learned, and the beauty of moments shared.

A STORM

A storm is more than just a weather event; it is a symbol of disturbance, change, and a powerful opposing force. When storms come, we rarely expect them, and so we are often unprepared. Yet within their chaos lies the promise of renewal: the cleansing rain, the stillness that follows thunder, and the clarity left in their wake.

I thought about this as I stood in the galley, gazing through the small window. The clouds outside seemed to darken and twist, alive with the force of the wind. The air was charged, and I could feel the hairs on the back of my neck rise. Then the captain's calm voice filled the cabin: "We're expecting some turbulence ahead, so please fasten your seatbelts and remain seated."

Moments later, the plane shuddered and lurched, pulling me hard against the seatbelt. Adrenaline surged through me, yet, strangely, beneath the chaos, I discovered a quiet stillness. It felt like a hidden reservoir of calm opening inside me. Paulo Coelho's words came to mind: *"Not all storms come to disrupt your life; some come to clear your path."* The truth of that quote struck me deeply. Storms, whether in the sky or in life, are not always sent to destroy. Sometimes they strip away obstacles, reveal what truly matters, and guide us toward paths we might not otherwise see.

When the turbulence finally eased and the seatbelt sign turned off, I reached for my phone and snapped a picture through the galley window. The clouds still loomed dark and frightening, breathing with life, a reminder of nature's raw power. Yet just beyond their edge, I caught sight of a brilliant sunset. The horizon blazed with orange and pink, a vision so breathtaking it seemed almost impossible after such darkness. That contrast moved me, a reminder that even in the heart of turmoil, beauty waits to be revealed and hope still flickers.

As the plane steadied against the storm, I reflected on how turbulence mirrors the unrest we face in our own lives. Challenges arrive suddenly, throwing us off balance and testing our resolve. Yet just as the sun breaks through heavy clouds, light eventually finds its way into our darkest moments. Storms, though unpredictable and often unwelcome, can be powerful catalysts for growth and transformation.

When the turbulence finally eased, and the seatbelt sign turned off, I exhaled a long breath I hadn't realized I was holding. Relief washed over me, but so did gratitude—for the calm, for the lesson, for the reminder that storms always pass. Haruki Murakami's words echoed softly in my mind:

"And once the storm is over, you won't remember how you made it through, how you managed to survive. You won't even be sure whether the storm is really over. But one thing is certain: when you come out of

the storm, you won't be the same person who walked in. That's what this storm's all about."

TOUGH SOLDIER ONBOARD

Even the briefest interactions can leave an imprint on our lives. Sometimes it is a short conversation, a small gesture, or an unexpected meeting that reveals courage, resilience, and the quiet strength of the human spirit. Working as a flight attendant, I have the privilege of meeting thousands of people. Most passengers pass by in a blur of boarding passes and carry-ons, but every so often, someone leaves a mark that lingers long after the flight is over.

One such moment came during a flight from Portland, Maine, to JFK, when I had the honor of meeting SSG Travis Mills. As he boarded with his father-in-law, I immediately noticed his amputation. Observation is part of our job, but in that instant, what struck me even more than his visible scars was the way he carried himself — calm, lighthearted, and without a trace of self-pity. They settled into their seats quickly, joking and playing a game on their phones, their laughter spilling into the cabin. It was clear that humor and connection were at the heart of how they faced life.

Travis Mills is a retired U.S. Army Staff Sergeant, motivational speaker, actor, author, and advocate for veterans and amputees. He also founded the Travis Mills Foundation, which supports post-9/11 veterans and their families as they adjust to life after injury. What struck me most is that he does not like to be described as wounded. Instead, he describes himself simply as *"a man with scars, living life to the fullest."*

Serving him that day was a privilege. Though I had noticed his amputation right away, I chose not to dwell on it. His openness and warmth immediately put me at ease as we spoke. He shared that they were headed to Las Vegas, Nevada, where he had a speaking engagement. Only then did I realize I was serving someone whose story had touched countless lives far beyond the cabin of our aircraft.

When we landed at JFK, Travis kindly handed me the first chapter of his book, *Tough as They Come*. In it, he writes:

"Never give up, never quit. Thousands of soldiers die each year to defend their country. United States Army Staff Sergeant Travis Mills was sure that he would become another statistic when, during his third tour of duty in Afghanistan, he was caught in an IED blast four days before his twenty-fifth birthday. Against all odds, he lived, but at a severe cost. Travis became one of only five soldiers from the wars in Afghanistan and Iraq to survive a quadruple amputation."

I sat with those words for a long time. Many of us cannot imagine the reality of what he endured: the sudden explosion, the searing pain, the long months of recovery, and the daily challenges of living with such profound injuries. Yet what stood out in his writing was not despair but determination. In his book, he insists, *"I'm just a man with scars, living life to the fullest and best I know how."*

That sentence has stayed with me. It is easy to see scars as reminders of loss, but he reframes them as proof of survival, strength, and purpose. His scars are not the end of his story but the beginning of a new one.

Encounters like this stay with me long after the flight is over. His quiet dignity, paired with his infectious sense of humor and unwavering optimism, left a deep impression on me. I realized that true toughness is not loud or forceful. Sometimes it looks like kindness. Sometimes it looks like choosing to smile when you could complain, or inspiring others when you would be justified in giving up.

I also thought about my own life and struggles, and how often I take the minor inconveniences of daily life too seriously. Compared to what people like Travis have endured, my difficulties seemed smaller, but not insignificant. His story did not make me dismiss my struggles. Instead, it motivated me to confront them with more gratitude and determination.

After that flight, I became more aware of the sacrifice and heroism of our soldiers and their families. It is easy to forget, while going about ordinary life, that freedom has a price, and that many pay it in ways the rest of us may never fully comprehend. The world is full of unsung heroes: soldiers, caregivers, survivors, and everyday people who carry invisible burdens yet choose to live with courage.

Travis Mills reminded me that we all have scars, whether visible or hidden. They may come from war, illness, heartbreak, or personal loss. But like him, we can choose how to carry them.

We can let them weigh us down, or we can let them tell a story of endurance, resilience, and hope.

As flight attendants, we often think our job is just about safety and service. But sometimes, our role is also to witness humanity in its rawest form. Meeting Travis Mills reminded me that behind every seat number and boarding pass is a story, often one of courage, sometimes one of pain, but always worth honoring.

It is up to us to listen, to learn, and to let their courage inspire our own path forward. And sometimes, it only takes a brief encounter, 35,000 feet above the ground, to remind us of the strength that lives within us all.

CELEBRITY DAY

S ome days at work stand out, shining brighter than others, etched in memory long after the flights are over. Today was one of those rare days—a day I can only describe as my "Celebrity Day." The name may sound fancy, but it captures how I felt as I moved through the cabin, surrounded by warmth and enthusiasm. Ordinary exchanges with passengers took on a glow, as if for a few hours I had stepped into a small spotlight. It wasn't about fame or status, but about joy shared, about being seen and appreciated in an unexpected way.

As a flight attendant, I've always valued the human connections that come with this role. Meeting people from diverse cultures, listening to their stories, and sharing moments of kindness are at the core of who I am. I also value photographs. To me, photos are not just images; they are memories stored in plain sight. I may forget the details of places or exact words spoken, but one glance at a photo brings everything back—the feelings, the laughter, the atmosphere. Research in the Journal of Personality and Social Psychology affirms this truth, showing how revisiting positive memories through photographs can boost happiness. That's why I keep taking them. Photography is not just a hobby but a way of stringing together fleeting experiences into something that endures. Every photo tells a story not only of where I've been but also of who I've met and the small sparks of connection we shared at 35,000 feet. Sometimes I wonder if, years from now, someone scrolling through their travel album will stumble upon a photo of me and smile at the memory of a kind encounter in the sky.

The funny thing is, today didn't begin with me feeling at my best. My hair felt off, my body was heavy with fatigue from a restless night of too much coffee, and my reflection didn't quite match the cheerful energy I wanted to carry. But it was the last day of my trip, what we call "go home day," and that thought kept my spirit positive, even if my body disagreed.

Then the unexpected happened. On our flight to Cincinnati, Ohio, not one but two passengers asked to take a photo with me. I've had occasional requests before, but never two in a single flight. Their enthusiasm reminded me of how important it is to remain approachable and genuine, even on days when I feel less than perfect.

The first was John, a dignified business traveler with a crisp yet casual style and a gentle smile. From the first-class cabin, he politely leaned in with a compliment and asked, "May I have a photograph with you to remember this flight?" His manner was so respectful that I couldn't help but smile and agree. I told him, "Certainly, but I prefer not to take selfies. When we land, I'll ask our captain to take it for us." True to my word, once we landed, I approached our captain with the request. Curious, he asked why I wanted a photo with John, and I chuckled as I corrected him: "Excuse me, Captain, it's the other way around—he wanted a photo with me!" We both laughed, the moment light and joyful.

Not long after John deplaned, a woman from Lagos, Nigeria, approached me. Her warm, radiant smile was unforgettable. She, too, asked if I would take a photo with her. By then, the exhaustion from the previous night had lifted. Her request felt like a gift—an affirmation that perhaps the small effort I put into greeting passengers with kindness truly left a mark. For me, it was another reminder that these candid snapshots and shared moments are the hidden treasures of this profession. They reflect to me what I sometimes forget: kindness and openness have a reach far greater than I can measure.

There is a special energy that comes with being acknowledged, not for fame, but for presence. It's the sense that the small, daily gestures we offer—smiles, kind words, patience—can ripple outward and touch people in ways we might never fully understand. Saying yes to a photo, pausing to share a laugh, or exchanging warm words can transform a fleeting interaction into something meaningful.

Every flight is filled with untold stories. Some are exchanged through conversation, others through photographs, and many remain unspoken yet deeply felt. These photographs are more than souvenirs; they are shared invitations to remember one another, to celebrate brief but genuine connections.

We cannot control how others perceive us, but we can choose to be authentic. Authenticity, I believe, is what draws people in. When we are comfortable in our own skin, people sense it. That belief guides me each day as I strive to show up as myself, even on days when I feel tired or imperfect.

Encounters like these remind me that my work goes beyond safety checks, serving meals, or making announcements. It is about creating moments that matter, moments that say to passengers: you are welcome, you are seen, you are valued. And sometimes, in return, passengers remind me of the same.

John and the woman from Lagos made me feel like a celebrity for a day, but more than that, they gave me the gift of recognition, not for appearance, not for glamour, but for presence, kindness, and authenticity. And that is the kind of spotlight I cherish most.

Not every day brings recognition, but when it does, it affirms what I already believe — that even the smallest gestures can ripple into something lasting. Sometimes, the photograph is not only for the passenger but also for me. A shared snapshot in time, a bridge between strangers, a reminder that kindness has a way of being remembered.

♥

SHE IS A WINNER

When people hear the word *winner*, they often think of trophies, medals, or applause. It is easy to associate winning with glory and recognition, but the true meaning of being a winner goes far deeper. Winning is found in resilience of spirit, in humility during triumph, and in the courage to face life's most difficult challenges.

During my journeys as a flight attendant, I have met many remarkable people, but some encounters linger long after the flight is over. On a trip to Boston, Massachusetts, I had the privilege of meeting Kelly Elmlinger. She was traveling to participate in a Paralympic competition, and when I asked for a photograph, she graciously agreed. At the time, I knew little about her, but later, as I learned her story, I was deeply moved by her journey.

Kelly is more than an athlete. She is a mother, a cancer survivor, a U.S. Army veteran, a full-time paratriathlete, and an Ambassador for the Wounded Warrior Project. Her life shows that winning is not about avoiding hardship, but about facing it and choosing to thrive in spite of it.

According to the Wounded Warrior Project, Kelly served 14 years on active duty and deployed three times to Afghanistan and Iraq as a medic. She routinely flew and drove to crash sites to evacuate wounded soldiers, displaying courage and selflessness in dangerous conditions. Later, when she faced her own battle with cancer, she brought the same determination to her personal fight.

Her role as a mother gives even greater depth to her story. TeamUSA.com highlights that her daughter, Jayden, is her greatest motivator. Kelly treasures the opportunity to shape her daughter's perspective and to show her that people with disabilities can accomplish the same things as anyone else. In this way, she not only inspires the public but also provides her child with a powerful example of strength and perseverance.

Her words in an interview with ESPN reflect the mindset that sustains her: "I'm big on potential. I know I have the potential, and I have to act on it." She never allowed herself to complain or feel sorry for what she was missing. Instead, she focused on what remained possible and acted with resolve. That is the heart of true resilience.

Meeting Kelly reminded me that true victory is not measured by medals. Whether she stood on the podium or not, she was already a winner. Her optimism, her persistence, and her ability to inspire others spoke more loudly than any accolade. Having her on our flight was a privilege, and my brief encounter with her reminded me that inspiration is not bound by circumstance but is shaped by choice.

The photograph I took with her now carries deep meaning. It reminds me not to dwell on my own limitations or minor struggles, but to face challenges with gratitude and strength. Kelly gave me a gift without realizing it: a lesson in courage that still influences how I approach life.

Her story shows that genuine strength emerges through perseverance and humility. Being a winner is not an exclusive title for the few who achieve great victories. It is a mindset that anyone can embrace, whether on the world stage or in the quiet battles of everyday life. We are winners when we rise again, when we encourage others, and when we face life with integrity.

Kelly Elmlinger is proof of that truth. She did not set out to inspire, yet her actions spoke louder than words, leaving an impression on all who met her. On that flight, she touched my life. Through her story, she continues to remind me that the essence of a true winner is not found in medals or applause but in the strength of the human spirit.

♥

ON JOURNALING

Encouragement can appear in the most unexpected places. Sometimes it is found high above the clouds, in a smile shared between strangers, or in a quiet message written on the page of a journal. A few heartfelt words, thoughtfully offered, can become a source of strength and inspiration for years to come.

Journaling has always been more than writing. It is a ritual of reflection. Each entry holds memories, dreams, and the hopes of tomorrow. For travelers and dreamers alike, a journal is both a record and a sanctuary. It is the place we return to when the world feels uncertain or when we simply need a reminder of why we keep moving forward.

On one of my flights, I met Jean, a young woman from Saudi Arabia studying English in the United States. Her dream was to become a social worker in her home country, and her determination immediately impressed me.

During the flight, she asked me to write something encouraging in her journal. I gladly agreed, feeling honored to contribute to her journey.

This is what I wrote:

"It was a pleasure to have you and your family on our flight from Detroit to JFK on December 2, 2015. I am genuinely impressed that you came to the U.S. to study English and pursue your dream of becoming a social worker. I wish you all the best in achieving your goals, and I have no doubt you will succeed in your career. I can envision you as a thriving social worker soon. Good luck, and stay motivated. We hope you enjoyed your flight with us. It was a delight to meet you, and thank you for asking me to do this."

Looking back, I realize how something as simple as writing in a journal can hold so much meaning. To Jean, it may have been a small gesture, but to me, it was a reminder of the quiet power of kindness.

Words have the ability to travel far beyond the moment they are spoken or written. They can become an anchor during times of uncertainty, a spark of motivation during seasons of doubt, and a reminder that someone believed in us.

I still remember Jean's smile as she read the message. I could see the warmth in her eyes, perhaps feeling that her dreams were not hers alone to carry, but were now witnessed and encouraged by another person. That smile stays with me, even years later.

Like Jean, I also keep a journal of my journeys. Mine is called *I Love Flying: An Inspirational Journal for Your Flying and Travel Adventures.* I created and published it during the COVID-19 era, when planes were grounded, and the skies were unusually quiet. Even when flying was not possible, my love for aviation and journaling gave me a way to capture memories and hold onto hope.

The world inside an airplane is a reflection of humanity itself. Each passenger carries not only luggage but also stories, challenges, and aspirations. When encouragement is exchanged, it builds a bridge across cultures, languages, and borders.

Jean's request taught me that encouragement does not need to be grand to be meaningful. Sometimes, a few sentences in a journal are enough to shift perspective and inspire resilience.

It showed me that the power of kindness lies in its simplicity, and its effects ripple far beyond the moment.

Even now, I hope that Jean continues her journey with strength and determination, just as I hope that my words still offer her reassurance when she needs it most. In offering her encouragement, I too was encouraged.

That is the beautiful reciprocity of kindness: it uplifts both the giver and the receiver.

High above the clouds, I am reminded again and again that inspiration can be shared in many forms. Sometimes it is a conversation, sometimes a gesture, and sometimes just a few words in a notebook. Whatever form it takes, it is always a reminder that our words have the power to help dreams take flight.

♥

AMERICAN FLAG ON BOARD

T here is a unique weight and respect that fills any space when the American flag is present. Its stars and stripes speak without words, carrying within them sacrifice, unity, and the determination of those who served.

I experienced this during a flight from Atlanta. A woman boarded carrying a flag that represented her late husband, a veteran who had recently been laid to rest. The flag, folded into a perfect triangle, rested gently in her arms. She cradled it with care, and the sight left me silent with respect.

As I watched her, I was struck not only by the solemn dignity of the moment but also by the quiet strength she embodied. Her grief was present, yet she carried the flag as though it was more than fabric, more than a symbol. It was her husband's story. It was his sacrifice.

Seeing the American flag on board a plane is rare for me. That day, it reminded me that behind every flag are countless lives, families, and journeys shaped by service. Each one carries a story of devotion and courage.

The freedom that Americans hold so dearly is not abstract. It is built on the selflessness of men and women who have served, and on the families who love and remember them.

For me, that flight became more than just a journey through

the skies. It was a quiet moment of reflection on sacrifice, honor, and the true meaning of freedom.

Thank you for your service, sir. This song goes out to you:

God Bless America
Land that I love.
Stand beside her, and guide her
Through the night with the light from above.
From the mountains, to the prairies
to the oceans, wide with hope
God Bless America
My home sweet home.
God Bless America
My home sweet home
God Bless America
From the mountains, to the prairies
to the oceans, wide with hope
God Bless America
My home sweet home.
God Bless America
My home sweet home.

Recognizing and honoring the veterans on board is something I am committed to doing on our flight. As we descended toward our destination, I felt deep gratitude for those who serve and for their loved ones who walk with courage in their absence.

♥

GERMAN LESSON

L anguages offer a unique view of culture and identity. They shape how we see the world and how we connect with others. A language is more than vocabulary and grammar; it is a bridge, one conversation at a time, drawing strangers closer and opening windows into unfamiliar lives.

I have always admired people who speak multiple languages. It amazes me how they can keep them separate in their minds, switching back and forth with ease. Growing up, I had a front-row seat to watch someone try. My mother once set her heart on learning German. She practiced with cassette tapes, repeating the words over and over until they became part of her daily rhythm. I, however, was less enthusiastic. At that age, German felt distant and complicated, and I never caught her passion for it.

Years later, during a flight, life handed me my own small German lesson. I met a family returning home to Germany: a mother traveling with her six-year-old twins, Carol and Cathy. From the start, the girls were unforgettable — bright, polite, and endlessly curious, with the kind of natural charm that makes you smile without realizing it.

As the plane climbed and leveled off above the sunlit clouds, Carol leaned forward in her seat, her eyes sparkling with questions. She reminded me of a young journalist, eager to uncover stories from the world around her. She asked me one question after another, and while I don't recall every single one, I will never forget the question that made me pause:

"How many languages do you speak?"

I laughed softly before answering, "I can only fluently speak two—English and Filipino. I know a little Spanish, too."

Carol tilted her head thoughtfully, as though she were filing the information away for a report. Then, in the way children do, she turned the moment into a game. She began teaching me German words right there in the aisle of an airplane. Her twin sister, Cathy, giggled at my pronunciation, and together they repeated the words until I got them right.

In return, I proudly shared my favorite German word: *Danke*. Simple, short, easy to remember. But the word carried a weight far greater than its syllables. In that moment, "Danke" was not just thanks—it was a connection.

The twins' energy was contagious. What began as a playful exchange of words soon turned into laughter and camaraderie. For a few minutes, the plane wasn't just filled with passengers traveling from one state to another; it was filled with the joy of discovery, the universal delight of learning something new.

When we finally parked by the gate, Carol, full of excitement, unbuckled her seatbelt. She jumped up, reached for my hand, and insisted I carry her. It caught me by surprise but also filled me with warmth. Her mother quickly snapped a photo of us together. That picture is now one of my favorites — a frozen memory of two little girls who reminded me of the beauty hidden in the simplest of encounters.

Later, as I walked through the airport, I kept thinking about Carol and Cathy. Their playful curiosity had turned an ordinary flight into something far more memorable. Their questions and their laughter left me reflecting on the richness of languages — not as a skill to master, but as a doorway into someone else's world.

Sometimes, all it takes is a single word to build that bridge. A child's eager "Danke" carries just as much meaning as a long conversation. Words hold power not in their complexity, but in the way they make another person feel seen and included.

Every time I visit Germany now, I think of those twins. I picture their eager faces, their voices teaching me new words, and their laughter as I stumbled through my German "lesson." That memory has become a gentle reminder: approach every new language, every culture, every experience with the same joy and openness I saw in them.

It turns out my mother was right all along. Learning a language is more than practice — it is an act of connection, a small invitation to step into someone else's world. And sometimes, the best teachers are six years old.

♥

GRANDMA AND GRANDSON TANDEM

T he grandson boarded our flight to New York with careful steps, his arm gently supporting an elderly woman whose face radiated pure joy. After weeks of recovery in Cincinnati, Ohio, his grandmother was finally well enough to return home, and their reunion celebration had clearly begun before they even found their seats.

"She's been asking about this flight for days," the grandson told me as they settled into their row. "Haven't you, Grandma?" She squeezed his hand and beamed at me with the kind of smile that instantly warms a room.

What struck me most was watching their easy rhythm together. Throughout the flight, he anticipated her needs without being asked—adjusting her pillow, sharing his magazine, quietly checking that her seatbelt wasn't too tight. She, in turn, filled every moment with stories that made him laugh, her eyes bright with the energy of someone who had fought through illness and won.

Their conversation created a bubble of warmth that seemed to extend beyond their seats. Other passengers glanced over, smiling at their obvious affection. During the beverage service, when I brought them their drinks, the grandmother raised her plastic cup with mock ceremony.

"To good health and even better grandsons!" she declared, making all three of us laugh.

Watching them reminded me that some of life's most meaningful journeys aren't about destinations—they're about who we travel with. The grandson's patient attentiveness and the grandmother's grateful joy created something beautiful together. In their shared glances and easy laughter, I saw the kind of intergenerational bond that weathers illness, distance, and time.

Their story stayed with me long after we landed. In our fast-paced world, where families are often scattered across cities and states, their reunion felt like a quiet rebellion against the forces that keep loved ones apart. It reminded me that caring for our elders isn't just about duty—it's about recognizing the wisdom and joy they still have to offer.

As I watched them walk arm-in-arm through the terminal, I realized their journey was already complete before the plane ever landed. They had what they came for: each other, health restored, and the unbreakable connection that turns any ordinary flight into a celebration of love.

♥

CHEERS TO THE AWARDEES

The energy was unmistakable from the moment they boarded our flight from Jacksonville, Florida, to New York. A group of Coach employees, all celebrating their company's annual recognition, practically bounced down the aisle with excitement that filled the entire cabin.

"We can't believe we actually won!" one of them told me, clutching her boarding pass like a golden ticket. Her colleagues nodded enthusiastically, their faces glowing with pride and anticipation.

Their joy was infectious. During the flight, they shared stories about their work, their gratitude for being recognized, and their plans for New York. When I served beverages, they insisted on making it a celebration.

"To Coach for believing in us!" one raised her plastic cup high."And to hard work paying off!" another added, grinning.

I couldn't help but join their impromptu toast. "Cheers and congratulations to the awardees!" we all said together.

Watching these employees celebrate reminded me of something I'd learned during my years in Human Resources:

recognition isn't just about the award itself—it's about feeling truly seen and valued. When companies take time to acknowledge individual achievements, they create something more powerful than motivation. They create belonging.

As a flight attendant, I've written countless compliment letters for colleagues who've gone above and beyond. I've seen how a simple acknowledgment from a passenger or supervisor can transform someone's entire trip. But there's something especially powerful about witnessing recognition on this scale— a company investing in celebration, bringing people together to honor their contributions.

The Coach employees' excitement stayed with me throughout the flight and long after we landed. Their story reminded me that in our daily routines, it's easy to forget how much we all crave acknowledgment. Whether it's a prestigious company award or a heartfelt "thank you" from a coworker, recognition creates ripples that extend far beyond the moment it's given.

These passengers reminded me that celebration amplifies achievement. Their shared joy didn't diminish because it was divided among them—it multiplied, and in doing so, inspired everyone around them.

♥

COMFORT DOLL

She held the small cloth doll close to her chest as turbulence rocked our flight over the Midwest. While other passengers gripped their armrests or checked their seatbelts, the woman in 14C simply adjusted her companion—a well-loved doll with faded features and a soft, worn face that spoke of countless journeys.

I'd noticed her during boarding, the way she carefully positioned the doll on her lap before even fastening her seatbelt. During the beverage service, curiosity got the better of me.

"That's a special travel companion," I said gently.

She smiled, her fingers tracing the doll's threadbare dress. "I've been flying with Sophie for eight years now," she explained. "I used to be terrified of flying, but one day I decided I wasn't going to let fear keep me grounded anymore. Sophie was my daughter's doll, and somehow holding her makes me feel like I can handle anything."

The doll's face showed the evidence of years of comfort—fabric slightly stained, eyes that had once been bright now softened with age, lips blurred from countless worried fingers seeking reassurance. To a stranger, Sophie might have looked shabby. To this woman, she was courage made tangible.

As we continued talking, I learned that Sophie had traveled to business meetings in twelve states, family reunions across the country, and even an international trip to see her daughter study abroad. Through delayed flights, emergency landings, and countless moments of uncertainty, this small cloth companion had been a constant source of calm.

Her story reminded me of my own childhood comfort pillow — dirty, misshapen, and precious beyond measure. My daughter Mary had one too, a small pillow she carried everywhere until she simply didn't need it anymore. We never threw those pillows away; they represented something too important to discard.

Watching this woman with Sophie, I realized that seeking comfort isn't about weakness — it's about wisdom. It's understanding ourselves well enough to know what we need to face our fears and move forward anyway. In a world that often demands we appear invulnerable, carrying a comfort object becomes a quiet act of self-care and honest self-awareness.

When we landed in New York, I watched her carefully place Sophie in her carry-on bag, the same tender attention she'd shown throughout the flight. As she walked down the jetbridge, I thought about all the ways we find courage — some through meditation, others through prayer, and some through the simple act of holding something soft and familiar while facing the unknown.

Her story stays with me because it illustrates a beautiful truth: sometimes the bravest thing we can do is admit we need comfort, and sometimes the strongest among us are those who aren't afraid to bring their vulnerabilities along on the journey.

DAFFODILS

There is a universal language in giving flowers to a stranger — an exchange that requires no words yet speaks volumes. A single blossom can soften a busy day, bridging the space between two people who may never meet again. The beauty isn't just in the petals themselves but in the gesture, in the reminder that kindness can arrive unexpectedly, wrapped in color and grace.

It happened on a flight to Minneapolis, Minnesota, when a woman with kind eyes and an easy smile handed me a small bundle of yellow daffodils. Their brightness seemed almost out of place in the narrow aisle of the airplane, and yet they belonged there in her hands. She offered them so naturally, as though giving flowers to a stranger when we landed was the most ordinary thing in the world. I couldn't help but smile as I accepted them. Her gift, so small and so thoughtful, lifted my spirits instantly.

Flowers carry meaning far beyond decoration. They comfort, they encourage, they celebrate, and sometimes they even heal. Among them, the yellow daffodil is the most cheerful. To many, it signals the arrival of spring, but to me it represents resilience — the courage to rise again after hardship, the promise of renewal, and the hope of brighter days.

Airports are full of flowers if you know where to look. I've seen them tucked carefully into carry-ons, cradled gently against chests, or peeking out of tote bags as passengers hurry toward their gates. A bouquet moves differently than luggage; it's handled with tenderness, as if everyone knows it carries more than petals. I often wonder about the stories behind them. Are they meant for a joyful reunion, an apology whispered at baggage claim, a birthday celebration, or a simple "just because"? Flowers, I think, are always more than they seem.

As I held those daffodils in my hands, their golden faces seemed to shine against the dull gray of the galley. They reminded me that compassion doesn't need grand gestures or carefully chosen words. It flourishes in small moments, when hearts are open to giving and receiving. Each blossom felt like it was offering its own quiet blessing: a promise of strength, of prosperity, of beauty that endures no matter the setting.

In the rush of travel — with its delays, its cramped cabins, and its constant motion — it is easy to forget the softness of human connection. But sometimes, all it takes is a few daffodils from a stranger to remind us to pause, to breathe, and to notice the goodness still blooming around us.

♥

TRUE DEDICATION

T rue dedication is rarely loud. It doesn't always arrive in the form of awards or grand gestures. More often, it reveals itself quietly — in steady hands, thoughtful choices, and the willingness to keep showing up, even when no one is watching.

In aviation, dedication means more than completing a checklist of duties. It is anticipating needs before they're spoken, supporting colleagues during long hours, sacrificing a bit of your own comfort, and taking pride in every detail of the journey you help create. It is found in the small moments as much as in the big ones.

I still remember a passenger, a frequent flyer with medallion status, who once approached me mid-flight. He said, "I fly four times a week, and you are the most dedicated flight attendant I've encountered." His words stayed with me — not because of the compliment itself, but because they came from someone who had seen countless crews and flights. For him to recognize something different reminded me that dedication isn't just about meeting expectations. It's about lifting the experience a little higher for others.

I also witnessed an unforgettable example of dedication from a ramp agent in Burlington, Vermont. It was pouring rain that day, the kind of weather that soaks everything in minutes. Before passengers began boarding, he carefully laid down blankets and wiped the wet floor at the main cabin door, making sure no one would slip as they entered. It wasn't his responsibility to go that far, but he did. His concern for the passengers' safety spoke volumes about his pride in his work.

When we love what we do, going the extra mile no longer feels like extra work. It becomes natural. And what's even more powerful is that dedication is contagious. When one person shows it—whether it's a gate agent calming anxious customers during a delay, a flight attendant racing against the clock to finish meal service on a short flight, or ramp crews braving icy winds to load cargo—it inspires those around them to rise to the same standard.

Dedication creates a ripple effect. A single act of care spreads outward, changing the tone of a workplace, the spirit of a flight, even the way passengers treat one another. I've seen it happen again and again: the kindness of one crew member or the thoroughness of one gate agent motivates others to match that energy. Together, those small acts weave into something bigger, something that passengers can feel the moment they step onboard.

Ultimately, what makes an exceptional team stand out is not only its skill or experience but also the collective willingness to serve wholeheartedly. Dedication, when it becomes the shared language of a crew, transforms challenges into opportunities and delays into moments of patience. It binds us together in the sky, reminding us that when we give our best, success naturally follows.

EMPATHY

Empathy often appears quietly, almost unnoticed at first, yet its effects ripple outward in ways that linger long after the moment has passed. It is more than simply understanding another person's feelings — it is the choice to adjust our own actions to ease their burden. On airplanes, where strangers sit shoulder to shoulder, empathy has the power to transform what could be an ordinary trip into a memory of human connection.

One late-night flight stays vivid in my mind. The cabin was hushed, most passengers settled into their seats with eyes closed, lulled by the steady hum of the engines. In the first-class section, a middle-aged man sat reading his book in the dark, holding the pages close to catch what little light spilled in from the aisle.

Leaning in gently, I asked him, "Can you see that clearly enough?" He looked up, gave me a small smile, but didn't answer right away. A moment later, he motioned to me and said softly, "Would it be all right if I moved back to an empty seat in Economy Comfort? That way I can turn on the light without disturbing anyone."

I assured him, "You don't need to move. You're welcome to turn on your reading light. Nobody around you is sleeping right now."

I paused, then my smile widened. "That's very kind of you," I said. "You're paying attention to how people might feel. Not everyone does that."

What struck me was not just his gratitude but the decision he had almost made. Here was a first-class passenger — someone who had paid for the comfort of a premium seat — willing to give it up so that others around him would not be disturbed. It was a simple, thoughtful choice, but it spoke volumes about the quiet power of empathy.

Empathy is rarely grand or dramatic. It shows itself in these subtle moments: when we notice another person's unspoken need, when we pause to consider how our actions might affect them, and when we choose kindness even if no one else will ever know. These small acts create warmth in spaces that might otherwise feel cold or impersonal, whether on an airplane or in daily life.

In a world that often emphasizes speed, efficiency, and personal gain, empathy can feel like a radical act. It takes awareness, patience, and a willingness to put others' comfort alongside our own. But when it appears — when someone lowers their voice, gives up their seat, shares a smile, or simply chooses to care — it becomes a thread in the larger fabric of humanity.

Reflecting on that late-night flight, I realized how far such a gesture can travel. The gentleman's willingness to adjust for others inspired me, and perhaps inspired those who witnessed it as well. That is how empathy works: it begins quietly, spreads gently, and reminds us that we are connected, even among strangers in the sky.

EVERYDAY SUNSHINE

T here is something magical about the phrase "everyday sunshine." It suggests more than just light; it speaks to the warmth, hope, and quiet brightness that one person can bring into the lives of others. Sometimes, those words arrive exactly when we need them most.

That morning in Montreal, Canada, I was rushing. Our hotel was conveniently inside the airport, but despite that, I found myself pressed for time. As I hurried toward security, I realized the line had stalled. Several passengers in wheelchairs needed extra assistance, and the process was moving slowly. My stress rose as the minutes ticked by. I pulled out my phone and called crew scheduling to let them know I might be a little late.

Stress is part of this job—sometimes sharp, sometimes fleeting. Over the years, I've learned that perspective makes all the difference. Standing there, I reminded myself to be patient, to notice what was happening instead of only focusing on the clock. The interactions in front of me were tender, filled with small gestures of care as agents helped the wheelchair passengers through. Watching that softened my own frustration, and I took a deep breath.

By the time I reached my gate, I paused to reset before

boarding. Morning sunlight spilled through the wide windows, washing the terminal in a soft golden glow. I let myself soak it in, as if the light itself was telling me to slow down, to carry something brighter into the day.

Once boarding began, the tension of the morning began to dissolve. The first wheelchair passenger came aboard, and I helped her settle into her seat. The second followed, and as he rolled into the cabin, he greeted me with a warm smile. "You're an everyday sunshine," he said. "I was on your flight to Montreal the other day."

His words stopped me in my tracks. Everyday sunshine. The compliment felt like a small gift, perfectly timed.

Later, after the flight, I sat by a window and watched sunlight stretch across the tarmac, steady and golden. It seemed to echo what he had said, reminding me that light comes in many forms. Sometimes it shines in the sky; sometimes it shines through words.

Being called "everyday sunshine" is one of the kindest compliments I've ever received. It reminded me that sunshine isn't guaranteed every day. There are cloudy mornings and stormy afternoons, days when stress takes over and perspective feels hard to hold. But storms always pass, and the sun eventually returns.

That's what kindness can do. A thoughtful word or simple gesture can shift the course of an entire day, dissolving stress and reminding us of our own capacity to bring warmth. The passenger's words traveled with me long after that flight, like sunlight breaking through clouds. And in return, I made a quiet promise to carry that brightness forward, to be someone's everyday sunshine whenever I could.

FEAR OF FLYING

I have learned that the fear of flying is not always loud or dramatic. Sometimes it is hidden behind a polite smile, a nervous laugh, or a question asked more for comfort than curiosity. "How long have the pilots been flying?" "What is the weather like today?" These little exchanges are often quiet ways of asking, "Am I safe?" Often, all it takes is a gentle word of reassurance or a moment of kindness to ease the weight of that fear.

Over the years, I have seen countless anxious passengers. Some tap their feet or grip the armrest until their knuckles turn white. Others tremble during turbulence, their voices unsteady when asking for water or reassurance. What has always struck me is how visible fear becomes in these moments. It is one of the rare instances where adults openly display their vulnerability in public.

On one flight, the gate agent pulled me aside and mentioned that a family of four would be boarding, and their daughter was terrified of flying. I expected a little girl, maybe six or seven. But when they arrived, I saw a young woman, already crying before she even reached the aircraft door. Her mother leaned in and said softly, "This is my daughter, Lea. She's afraid of flying."

Her face carried sheer panic, and my heart went out to her instantly. My name was so close to hers that I felt an instant bond. I stopped what I was doing and gave her my full attention. "Captain," I called, "we have Lea here, and she's an anxious flyer. Do you have a moment to talk with her?"

I turned back to her with a calm smile. "You don't need to be afraid, Lea. Our pilots are highly skilled, and our captain has been flying for many years. You are in good hands." She listened, though her tears still fell. The captain came over and invited her into the cockpit. His steady voice carried the kind of reassurance I hoped she needed. "I've been flying for over twenty years," he told her. "You'll be safe with us." Her mother even took a photo of the moment, a keepsake of the kindness extended to her daughter.

During the flight, I gave Lea a pair of flight attendant wings and slipped her a handwritten note with a few words of encouragement. I told her that fear doesn't always last forever and that every flight could bring her one step closer to courage. Her mother thanked me again, her relief as visible as her daughter's earlier fear.

By the time we landed, Lea seemed calmer, her shoulders no longer drawn so tightly. As her family deplaned, I found myself reflecting on how it is not only turbulence or delays that mark a journey. Sometimes, the truest victories in the sky are small and quiet—the eased breath of a nervous traveler, the smile that replaces tears, or the courage found in the space between fear and trust.

I hope that on Lea's next flight, she will carry not dread but excitement, and that when she looks out above the clouds, she will remember that fear can be softened by kindness and courage can grow when it is shared.

Here are some ways to help you conquer the fear of flying:

- Educate yourself, get familiar with, and understand how airplanes work, and the safety measures in place.
- Talk to the crew and let them know you're afraid of flying.
- Practice deep breathing exercises.
- Read books or magazines, watch movies, or listen to music to occupy your mind.
- Share your fears with friends or family.
- Arrive early at the airport to reduce stress from rushing.
- Avoid caffeine and sugary food.
- Stay hydrated.
- Bring comfort items such as a neck pillow, blanket, stress ball, or essential oils.
- Choose a seat over the wings where turbulence is felt less.
- Reaching out to family and friends before takeoff.
- Use relaxation or meditation Apps and positive affirmations.
- Watching videos of planes taking off and visiting an airport for exposure.
- If your fear is severe, seek professional help.
- Focus on the destination.

Each step you take towards conquering this fear is a victory, leading you closer to experiencing the freedom and joy of air travel.

FILIPINOS ON BOARD

As flight attendants, we meet thousands of passengers, but there's always something special about seeing a fellow Filipino on board. A smile, a familiar accent, or a greeting in Tagalog can instantly turn a routine flight into something personal. For Filipinos living abroad, these small, unexpected connections feel like home — like a warm thread weaving us back to our roots.

On a flight from Dallas, Texas, to JFK, I experienced one of those moments. As I made my way down the aisle, I noticed a couple with the unmistakable warmth of Filipinos. Mr. and Mrs. Molina greeted me with kind smiles that felt instantly familiar. They were traveling to the Holy Land, a destination also on my bucket list. With a mix of pride and surprise, Mr. Molina said, "We've been traveling for nearly 30 years and have never had a Filipina flight attendant on our flights. This is our first experience with you."

I was honored to be that first. In all those decades of flying, they had never crossed paths with someone from their own heritage in uniform. That realization made the moment even more meaningful.

As we chatted, I learned that Mr. Molina had served 20 years in the military. I thanked him sincerely for his service. Then, with the quiet generosity that Filipinos are known for, Mrs. Molina reached into her bag and offered me a sweet treat— *Goldilocks polvoron* from the Philippines. That simple gesture touched me deeply. It reminded me of home, of family, and of the unspoken bond that connects Filipinos no matter where in the world we meet.

Encounters like these remind me why I treasure meeting *kababayans* on flights. Their stories of travel and of the Philippines reconnect me to my heritage. More importantly, I admire the humility that shines through people like Mr. and Mrs. Molina. Sometimes, social status and success can cause us to forget where we came from, but those who remain humble are the ones who leave the strongest impression.

That day, the Molinas reminded me of something I try to carry with me always: every journey is not just about the destination but also about the people we meet along the way. And when those people reflect your own culture and values to you, the flight becomes more than travel—it becomes a memory you carry long after landing.

FUTURE AVIATORS

T he dream of flying often begins with small, unforgettable moments: a first trip on an airplane, the thrill of hearing engines roar to life, or the magical view from a cockpit window. For many children, that spark of wonder becomes the seed of a lifelong passion.

On one of my recent flights, I met three young women who carried that same spark in their eyes. Their curiosity and excitement reminded me of how aviation dreams are born. When I mentioned that I could arrange for them to visit the cockpit after landing, their faces lit up instantly. They leaned forward, whispering to one another, their anticipation impossible to hide.

After we touched down, the captain welcomed them into the cockpit. I watched as they carefully stepped inside, wide-eyed at the glowing instruments and the view of the runway stretching out ahead. One of them traced a finger along her pilot's wing pin, which I had given her earlier, and smiled as if she were already imagining herself in uniform one day. In that small space, with the hum of quiet engines around us, I could almost see the future of aviation standing before me.

It struck me how powerful these experiences can be. A brief

glimpse behind the scenes, a wing pinned to a shirt, or a kind word of encouragement may be all it takes to ignite a lifelong dream. Though they may still be exploring their career paths, moments like this have the power to plant a vision that stays with them forever.

Aviation has long been seen as a male-dominated field, but that is steadily changing. More women are stepping into roles as pilots, mechanics, and leaders within the industry. Each year, their numbers grow, and their presence inspires others to believe that the sky is open to everyone.

As I watched those three young women leave the plane, chatting excitedly with their wings pinned proudly to their shirts, I felt hopeful. Whether they become pilots, mechanics, or flight attendants, I know they will carry this memory with them. Perhaps one day they will look back and remember the moment they first stepped inside a cockpit—and realize that was where their journey began.

The future of aviation is bright, and it lives in the eyes of dreamers like them.

♥

A STICKER AND A HUG

Sometimes, the smallest tokens carry the deepest meaning. A sticker, bright and playful, may look ordinary to most, but in the hands of a child, it becomes a symbol of trust, kindness, and connection. Children, in their innocent wisdom, often teach us more than we expect. Their gestures are pure, unfiltered by hesitation or the need for recognition, and they invite us to pause and share in their joy.

On a flight from LaGuardia to Raleigh-Durham, North Carolina, I met a mother traveling with her three young daughters — Bella, eight; Julie, seven; and little Jane, who trailed closely behind her sisters. From the moment they boarded, their sweetness filled the cabin. Bella had the quiet confidence of the oldest child, Julie carried a playful spark, and Jane clung to her mother's hand but smiled shyly whenever I caught her eye.

Their mother explained that they were moving permanently from Connecticut to North Carolina. I thought about the weight of such a change: packing up memories, saying goodbye to familiar places, and stepping into the unknown. Yet she carried herself with grace and calm, guiding her daughters with a steady hand and gentle patience. Traveling alone with three children could not have been easy, but she made it look effortless.

Midway through the flight, Julie pulled out her sticker booklet. She worked carefully, peeling back corners and smoothing stickers onto the page with the seriousness of an artist. Then, without hesitation, she chose one and handed it to me. "This is for you," she said with a grin. I placed it proudly on my dress and wore it for the rest of the flight. In return, I pinned a set of flight attendant wings onto each girl's shirt. Their eyes widened as though I had given them treasures.

That exchange stayed with me. A sticker and a pair of wings may be small things, but they carried weight. They were symbols of kindness freely given, tokens of connection shared in a moment of transition. For their mother, this trip was not just about flying to a new state but about leading her family into a new chapter. Watching how respectful and polite her daughters were, I could see her dedication reflected in them. It takes immense strength to raise children who carry such joy and good manners into the world.

As the captain announced our descent, the girls pressed their faces to the windows, eager to glimpse their new home. I wondered what was running through their mother's mind. Was she worried about what awaited them? Was she hopeful? Perhaps both. In her quiet composure, I saw the resilience of a woman determined to make the best of change for the sake of her children.

Just before deplaning, Julie wrapped her arms around me in a hug that was both unexpected and unforgettable. Her mother thanked me warmly, her gratitude evident not just in her words but in her expression, in the way she stood a little taller, reassured that kindness still met her family even in transit.

As I watched them walk down the jetbridge, sticker still on my dress, I realized that sometimes courage is revealed not in loud declarations but in the smallest acts. A sticker, a hug, a smile, or a helping hand can transform a moment, reminding us that new beginnings are made brighter through kindness.

"I LOVE YOU"

Some encounters linger in the heart long after the moment has passed. They begin quietly, like a whisper, and then expand into memories that stay with us, reminding us of what truly matters. I experienced such an encounter on a quiet flight when I met an older woman whose warmth and grace seemed to fill the entire cabin.

She had soft gray hair neatly brushed back, and her smile carried both gentleness and strength. Her movements were careful, but her spirit was steady. Though she struggled with hearing, her eagerness to connect shone brighter than any limitation. I affectionately called her Ms. Lovely. She was traveling alone to Baltimore, Maryland, to visit her son, and she seemed delighted to have someone to share her journey with.

We sat together for a while, exchanging stories. She spoke about her family with a tenderness that lit up her eyes. Each word reflected gratitude—gratitude for her children, for the chance to travel, for the blessings of health that still allowed her to move about the world. I found myself slowing down, leaning closer, not just to hear her better but to honor her presence. In a world that often rushes past the elderly, taking time to listen felt like a gift, both for her and for me.

Aging, I realized in that moment, is not only natural but beautiful. To grow older and still have the courage to travel, to stay curious, to carry stories and share them with others—this is a blessing. It reminded me that while bodies may slow, the soul carries wisdom, humor, and love that deserve to be seen and celebrated.

What struck me most was how much she gave without even trying. Ms. Lovely taught me that love is not confined to grand declarations. It thrives in the little things—a shared laugh, a gentle touch, a story told from the heart. The kind of love she radiated was unhurried and unconditional, the kind that quietly fills a space and leaves it warmer than before.

When the flight ended, and we waited together for her wheelchair, she turned to me with eyes full of affection. Leaning closer, she whispered, almost shyly, "I love you."

The words caught me off guard. In all my years of flying, I had never heard them spoken so tenderly by a passenger. They were simple, yet they carried the weight of sincerity and connection. In that instant, the noise of the airport around us seemed to fade.

I felt tears rise to my eyes, though I willed them back with a smile. I leaned down, hugged her gently, and whispered back, "I love you, too."

That fleeting exchange has stayed with me, not because it was dramatic or expected, but because it revealed the heart of human connection. Amid the bustle of travel, between security lines and boarding calls, love had quietly shown up in its purest form.

Even now, whenever someone says "I love you" unexpectedly, I think of Ms. Lovely. I remember her soft smile, her gentle words, and the courage it took to share them. She reminded me that in a world rushing from one destination to the next, the most important journeys are the ones that happen in our hearts. And sometimes, all it takes is three simple words to light the way.

♥

MR. BRUCE AND HIS ICE CREAM

I t's not every day that ice cream becomes the center of an unforgettable travel story. What began as a casual conversation in the cabin turned into one of the funniest encounters of my career—a moment that reminded me how even the simplest things, like a sweet tooth, can spark genuine connection.

On our flight from Atlanta to Havana, Cuba, I met a gentleman in first class whose personality was as bright as his smile. I was chatting with another passenger about living in Jacksonville, Florida, and about my plans to explore Havana. The gentleman leaned in with the ease of someone who enjoyed conversation and asked, "Have you ever tried Bruster's ice cream?"

I admitted with a laugh, "I've seen where it is, but I haven't tried it yet."

Without missing a beat, he grinned and said, "Oh, you really should give it a try!"

The way he insisted made me curious, though I didn't think much of it at first. After landing in Havana, the passengers began to deplane down the stairs. Just as this gentleman reached the bottom, he turned back with a booming voice and a huge smile and called out, "You really should try Bruster's ice cream. I'm Bruce!"

It took me a second to realize what had just happened. I burst out laughing. This wasn't just any friendly passenger giving a recommendation—this was *Mr. Bruce himself,* the owner of Bruster's Ice Cream, sneaking in the most charming, unexpected sales pitch I had ever heard. Suddenly, the whole conversation made sense.

Mr. Bruce's humor and energy were contagious. There was something delightful about the way he introduced himself—not with a business card or a serious handshake, but with a playful shout on an airplane staircase. It was a moment so lighthearted and genuine that it stuck with me long after the flight.

Encounters like this remind me of one of the greatest gifts of this job: meeting fascinating people from all walks of life. Some teach us, some inspire us, and some, like Mr. Bruce, simply make us laugh in a way we won't forget. I have no doubt he has made countless people smile, not only with his ice cream but also with his joyful spirit.

I still smile when I think about him and his impromptu pitch. One day, I hope to see him again—this time to tell him I finally tried his ice cream and loved it. And who knows, maybe I'll even ask if that first scoop comes with a flight attendant discount.

♥

IS SHE CRYING?

A mother's sacrifice is often quiet, stitched into the fabric of everyday life in ways that are easy to miss. She sets aside her own desires, rearranges her plans, and sometimes pauses her dreams for the sake of her children. Her devotion shows up not only in the grand milestones but in the countless little moments: a soothing word whispered after a nightmare, a gentle hug after a long day, laughter over a silly joke, or the patient way she listens when her child's small world feels overwhelming. Yet even in all the joy of giving, her heart carries an ache when separated from her child, no matter how brief the distance.

I was reminded of this truth one afternoon as our plane lifted off the ground. Sitting across from me on the jumpseat was a woman with her head tilted slightly toward the window. As the clouds shifted past, I noticed her discreetly wiping her eyes. Her expression was far away, as though her thoughts were traveling on a different path than the plane itself. For a moment, I simply wondered: *what story hides behind her tears?*

Once we reached cruising altitude, I unbuckled and approached her. "I noticed you wiping your eyes," I said softly. "Were you crying?"

She looked up, a little embarrassed but honest. "Yes," she admitted. "It's my first time traveling without my one-and-a-half-year-old daughter. She's at home with her dad. My husband gave me a break to attend a reunion." Her voice wavered, then brightened as she pulled out her phone to show me a photo of her husband holding their baby girl.

I smiled and reassured her. "She'll be fine. Your husband will take good care of her. You deserve to enjoy your reunion." Her shoulders eased as she thanked me, her smile small but genuine.

As the flight continued, I found myself watching her in quiet intervals. She seemed more at peace, scrolling through her phone, her eyes softening as if she were holding her family close through memory and love. Even in her longing, I sensed gratitude — gratitude for her daughter, her husband, and the gift of rediscovering a piece of herself outside of motherhood.

It struck me then: vulnerability doesn't weaken a mother's strength. It reveals it. A mother may ache in separation, yet she carries resilience in her willingness to keep loving fiercely, even when apart.

Behind every mother's smile, there may be a quiet ache of missing her child. And yet, in that ache, there is beauty. It is the proof of love. Mothers are naturally selfless, often putting their children's needs above their own, and still finding the courage to embrace small freedoms when life offers them.

As we began our descent, I reflected on the woman across from me. Her tears were not weakness, but love spilling over.

They were the kind of tears that tell the story of what it means to give, to let go, and to trust. In her vulnerability, she carried the quiet bravery of all mothers—a reminder that even in longing, love always remains the strongest thread.

LUGGAGE RIDDLE

T he day began like any other, with the hum of excitement in the air and the familiar shuffle of passengers preparing to board. But amid the ordinary, there's always a hint of mystery waiting to be discovered. And on this particular morning, a truly memorable passenger arrived.

A charming elderly gentleman was the first to board, and my eyes were drawn to his vintage, yet beautiful, pink luggage. The handle bore the marks of decades of journeys and countless stories, each scratch and scuff a testament to the adventures it had seen. I couldn't help but wonder where it had been and what tales it could tell.

My excitement and admiration for the luggage got the better of me, and I asked if we could take a photo with him and his treasured possession. His response was priceless: a warm yes and a big smile. I quickly grabbed my phone, and we posed, showing off the luggage. It was a moment of pure joy, and I couldn't help but feel a connection to this gentleman and his luggage.

As we chatted, I wondered if the luggage belonged to him. The journalist in me kicked in, and I asked where he got it. He confessed, with a twinkle in his eye, "This is my mother's luggage." I joked, "I would love to take it home!" We all shared a hearty laugh, and for a moment, it felt like we were the only ones in the cabin.

After our laughter faded, the gentleman's eyes sparkled with a touch of nostalgia. Maybe he was hearing echoes of his mother's laughter, or perhaps he was reminiscing about the adventures they'd shared. Throughout the flight, he sat contentedly in his seat, a soft smile lingering on his face. I imagined the places the luggage had been, the stories it could tell, and the memories it held.

As the plane began to taxi down the runway, my thoughts kept drifting back to the vintage luggage quietly resting in the overhead bin. Watching the gentleman sit so peacefully, I realized that he carried not only his belongings but also a piece of his family's history – a link to his mother's love and journeys. The luggage seemed to shimmer with the weight of memory, its genuine leather holding secrets of reunions and goodbyes, love letters, old photographs, and souvenirs from different cities and countries.

As we landed, I realized that at airports, amid the rush, we sometimes discover small treasures. This encounter reminded me that every flight, every journey, is full of stories, both old and new. The gentleman's luggage was more than just a piece of luggage – it was a tangible connection to his past, a reminder of the love and memories that shape us.

THE MAGIC WAND

There's something enchanting about the idea of a magic wand filled with limitless possibilities. This object connects hope and reality, making the impossible feel within reach. With just a flick, the air itself could shine with a new promise. As adults, we often yearn for that spark of magic – a sudden change in fortune, a chance meeting, or a gentle push that lifts us beyond our daily routines.

I had a wonderful conversation with a kind elderly man who was using a cane, and I helped him put it away. I jokingly told him I would use his cane as my magic wand. He burst into laughter, and his eyes lit up. In that moment, I realized that our exchange was more than just a playful conversation – it was a spark of connection, a shared moment where imagination bridged the gap between two strangers. He let me borrow the cane for a photo, and I waved the magic wand, making a wish for both of us.

As I reflect on that moment, I realize that a magic wand isn't just about granting wishes or fixing problems. True magic lies not in the object itself but in our ability to see wonders in everyday life. When we share a smile, offer help, or say a prayer, we create small miracles that spread outward. These simple acts, born from kindness, become the spells we cast to lift not only our spirits but those of others as well.

In moments of doubt or exhaustion, I look for signs – such as sunlight breaking through a cloudy sky, a friend's laughter, or an unexpected blessing – that feel almost magical in their timing, like a magic wand. These moments remind me that we can create our own version of magic, not with a physical object, but with the power of our words, vision, dedication, perseverance, and faith.

We don't need a fairy tale or a magic wand to unlock limitless possibilities. We can generate magic in our own lives, turning dreams into reality through the choices we make and the actions we take. It's not about waving a wand; it's about harnessing the power within us to create positive change. And sometimes, all it takes is a simple act of kindness to make the impossible feel possible.

♥

LITTLE REINDEER

Sometimes the smallest tokens carry the greatest weight. A worn photograph tucked into a wallet, a child's drawing folded neatly in a purse, a stuffed toy nestled inside a carry-on — these little treasures act as bridges between people. They hold quiet reminders of love, anchoring us when we are far from home and keeping our hearts tied to the ones who wait for us.

It was Christmastime, that season when airports are filled with the glow of decorations and the familiar symbols of the holidays — Santa Claus, twinkling lights, Christmas trees, and reindeer. The air felt both busy and tender, filled with travelers rushing to see loved ones. During those long trips away from home, even a little reindeer can mean more than tinsel or garlands. It can symbolize family, memory, and the comfort of belonging.

After landing in Milwaukee, Wisconsin, I noticed a man standing in the aisle. In his hands, he carried a small plush reindeer. With a quiet kind of reverence, he placed it gently on the headrest of his seat and pulled out his phone to take a photo. The sight caught my attention immediately. There was something so endearing, almost childlike, in that small act. I couldn't help but smile, curious about the story behind it.

I struck up a conversation. "That's a cute reindeer," I said warmly. "I love taking photos of little things on the plane, too."

He returned my smile, his eyes lighting up. "This is my daughter's toy. I bring it with me on my trips. Every time I land, I take a picture of it and send it to her and my wife." His voice carried both pride and tenderness.

In that moment, I saw more than a man with a stuffed animal. I saw a father who refused to let distance dull the bond with his family. Each snapshot was a love letter disguised as a photo—a promise whispered across miles. It said, *I made it safely. I'm thinking of you. I'll be home soon.*

I told him how sweet it was, and I meant it. Not many people take the time to carry such a tradition, and I could easily imagine the joy his wife and daughter felt each time his message arrived. What they received was not only a picture of a reindeer but a reassurance of his love, his thoughtfulness, and his presence even while far away.

As he tucked the little reindeer back into his bag with surprising care, I realized how these rituals create invisible threads of connection. Planes may carry us across continents and oceans, but it's often something small—a stuffed toy, a note, a keepsake—that keeps us close to home.

In a world that celebrates grand gestures, we sometimes overlook the quiet traditions that sustain love. But it's these daily rituals that matter most. They are living reminders that love doesn't fade with distance. It thrives in small acts, repeated faithfully, woven into our routines.

That day, the little reindeer wasn't just a toy. It was a companion, a messenger, and a promise. Proof that sometimes, love travels best in the smallest of packages.

And at Christmastime, when reindeer are most often imagined pulling sleighs through the night sky, this one reminded me of something just as magical. Love doesn't need wings or antlers to fly—it only needs intention. With every picture he sent home, that little reindeer became his family's symbol of hope, joy, and the sweetest gift of all: the promise of togetherness.

♥

LOST AND FOUND

Sometimes, the most unforgettable journeys are shaped not by the destinations we reach but by the challenges we face along the way. For me, a routine trip in April 2015 would become a test of resilience, turning each moment into a lesson learned and every setback into a story worth sharing.

It started in Detroit, Michigan, where I had a layover before deadheading to LaGuardia. I grabbed a quick salad at Wendy's, carrying only my wallet – a decision that would soon prove to be a costly mistake. Later, I boarded the plane to New York, unaware that my wallet was no longer with me. The next morning, as we prepared to depart from LaGuardia to Montreal, Canada, panic set in when I realized my wallet was missing. Inside, my green card, also known as a permanent resident card, was nestled alongside my other essentials. I retraced my steps, suspecting I'd left it on the counter at Wendy's while signing the receipt. Anxiety washed over me like a wave, and my mind began to race with worst-case scenarios.

My first step was to contact crew scheduling to see if I could fly without my green card. The staff reassured me that I could, as long as I had my passport. Though I'd been flying for less than a year and wasn't entirely sure of the policy, I decided to proceed based on their guidance. But little did I know, this was just the beginning of a series of challenges that would test my resolve.

Upon arrival in Montreal, I explained my situation to the immigration officer. To my relief, she let me into the country, and I was grateful for her understanding. However, the reprieve was short-lived. The next morning, our flight to JFK was scheduled for 5:00 AM, and what I expected to be a peaceful start quickly turned stressful. At the immigration counter, my heart pounded with hope and anxiety as I handed over my passport and explained my situation. The officer directed me to a waiting area, his words cutting deep: "You should not have been permitted to enter Montreal, and this error cannot be rectified with another." The weight of his words felt like a heavy burden, and I wondered if I'd ever make it back to the States without a hitch.

As the officer was on the phone, I quietly tried calling my manager, Karl, hoping he'd answer. The officer noticed me using my phone and warned me that I wasn't allowed to use it in that area. Fortunately, Karl answered, and I felt a glimmer of hope. He assured me he'd contact our company's security officer, and after a few tense minutes, the officer returned my passport. Endeavor Air had reached an agreement with their supervisor, allowing me to leave Montreal without the $500 fine. However, I was warned that a repeat offense would result in the company covering the cost – a stark reminder of the gravity of the situation.

As I left the interrogation room, exhaustion and relief washed over me, and tears welled up in my eyes. Initially, I felt helpless, but gradually, I appreciated my company's support during that tough time. Walking through the terminal, I became more cautious with each step. The airport, usually a place of routine, had transformed into a setting where vulnerability and compassion took center stage. I reminded myself that I wasn't alone amid the chaos – a truth that would become a lifeline in the days to come.

On the plane, the crew sensed my unease and offered reassurance, helping to stabilize my nerves as we prepared to depart. Despite the incident, we took off, albeit 30 minutes late. I took responsibility and humbled myself, acknowledging the gravity of the situation. When we arrived at JFK, Karl approached me on the plane, discreetly handing me some money. "Lia, take this $20, so you have some cash for the rest of your trip," he said. His kindness comforted me during that difficult time, and I felt a deep sense of gratitude towards him and the company.

For the next week, I held onto hope that my lost wallet would be returned. Replacing my green card would cost $500, a hefty price to pay. I kept checking my phone, eager for news. Then, the call came – Delta had found my wallet. I retrieved it, along with my green card, but the few dollars were missing. I was grateful to the person who found it and took the time to send it to the airport's Lost and Found. Miracles do happen, and faith endures – a truth that I would carry with me long after this ordeal was over.

This experience taught me valuable lessons: not to keep all my cards in one wallet, to stash some cash in my purse, and to always double-check my belongings. More importantly, it reminded me that compassion can come unexpectedly and that vulnerability, though uncomfortable, fosters humility and opens the door for grace to grow. The ripple effect of everything that happened stayed with me, a constant reminder that resilience can grow through uncertainty and adversity. Even in the most tense moments, there's room for hope and wisdom – a truth that I would carry with me for the rest of my journey.

MANIFESTATION PARTNER

Manifestation, a word that resonates deeply with me, is the process of using thoughts, feelings, beliefs, and actions to turn ideas into reality. It's the art of co-creating with the universe, where our intentions and energies align to bring forth our desires. A manifestation partner is more than just a friend or confidant; they're someone with whom you share your goals, dreams, and intentions, supporting each other on the journey to manifest them. This partnership thrives on trust, encouragement, and the shared energy of mutual belief.

When two people openly share their visions and align their energies, something powerful begins to emerge. The process is not without its challenges, though – doubts, setbacks, and sometimes the urge to give up. But together, manifestation partners serve as mirrors and motivators, reminding each other of their inner strength and the possibilities ahead. They celebrate each other's successes and offer support during times of uncertainty.

I had the privilege of experiencing this firsthand with my friend Cindy. We discovered that we both believed in the power of manifestation and shared experiences and techniques to strengthen our understanding of this powerful practice. As her birthday approached, I gave her a gift that would become a meaningful moment in our manifestation journey together – a new pair of work shoes. She expressed her gratitude and happiness, sharing that she had been manifesting the gift I had given her. I was surprised and pleased, feeling fulfilled to be part of her manifestation.

Moments like these remind me how powerful our intentions are in shaping our desires. Being part of someone else's manifestation journey is a meaningful experience, and I look forward to many more moments like this. I've learned that manifestation isn't a solo activity; its magic grows when celebrated and supported together. Having a manifestation partner means celebrating small wins and gently helping each other stay on track when doubts cloud our vision.

The law of attraction works better when we feel positive and grateful. Our energy vibrates at a higher, positive frequency, attracting experiences that resonate with our intentions. I've seen many of my desires come true and am actively working to manifest even more.

Through my journey, I've discovered some valuable tips and secrets for manifestation:

- Practice gratitude every morning to set a positive tone for the day.
- Replace negative thoughts with positive ones to shift your energy.
- Believe that good things are about to happen, and watch your reality unfold.
- Meditate for five minutes a day to connect with your

inner self.

- Create a vision board to visualize your desires.
- Visualize your goals and dreams with clarity and purpose.
- Start journaling to reflect on your progress and growth.
- Use positive affirmations to reprogram your mind.
- Consider your dreams before bed, allowing your subconscious to work its magic.

We have the power to create the life we want through manifestation. With consistency, these habits turn dreams into real progress. Even on tough days, trust that manifestation quietly molds our reality, one intention at a time. The journey is just as important as the destination, and with a manifestation partner by your side, the path becomes more enjoyable and rewarding.

♥

MEETING MR. CHARLES

Sometimes, a single encounter can become a story that lingers in your soul — an unexpected moment that shifts your perspective forever. One of such encounters began just like any other day, a routine flight tucked within the usual blur of busy travel. But I had no idea that today would bring with it a quiet lesson — one about empathy, responsibility, and showing up when it matters most.

That morning, during a brief conversation with our captain, he shared something that struck a chord: *"Some individuals endure their struggles quietly."* I didn't realize then how deeply those words would echo by the end of the day.

We were scheduled to fly from Burlington, Vermont, to JFK. As I stepped onto the plane, something in the air felt different — an odd undercurrent of curiosity and unease. Maybe it was intuition. Perhaps it was something more. But in hindsight, I believe the universe sometimes nudges us toward people who need us, even if we don't know why at the time.

That's when I met **Mr. Charles**.

He was in a wheelchair — frail, likely in his seventies, and moving with the kind of care that makes you look twice. His limbs didn't seem fully cooperative, as if each step cost him something. I helped him to his seat and assisted with his belongings. He thanked me gently, his voice carrying a softness that hinted at exhaustion.

During the flight, I noticed his hands trembled as he tried to eat. When we spoke, his words came slowly, tinged with a faint slur. I remembered the captain's words again. This — this man, quietly navigating his own private storm — was living proof of them.

I observed him throughout the flight, not intrusively, but attentively. There was something about him — his vulnerability, his quiet gratitude — that held my focus. When we landed at JFK, a wheelchair was waiting to take him to his connecting flight to Portland, Oregon. The other flight attendant and I helped with his carry-on and made sure he had everything he needed. I wished him well and moved on, assuming our interaction had come to an end.

But fate had other plans. As I headed toward my next flight, I noticed a small crowd gathering near one of the boarding gates. Curiosity drew me closer — and there he was: **Mr. Charles**, surrounded by onlookers. We were told to stay clear, so I couldn't approach him. Medical staff soon arrived and escorted him to Jamaica Hospital. He hadn't made his flight.

A sudden weight settled on me. I couldn't stop replaying our interaction. His trembling hands. His slow, quiet speech. His fragile frame. I imagined him alone now, in a hospital room far from home, with no way to contact family. Was he okay? Did his family know what had happened? Would someone call them?

I couldn't shake the feeling that I had a responsibility. Not as part of my job—but as a fellow human being. So, I acted. I returned to the Burlington flight gate and asked the gate agent for his contact information. She shared it with me, and I made several calls until I finally reached him the next day. His voice sounded weak, but he was conscious. I told him I would visit him that day at the hospital. I even offered to fly with him to Portland if he needed support.

That decision—small to some, risky to others—wasn't made lightly. As I weighed my responsibilities as a flight crew member against my desire to help, I faced an uncomfortable truth: Sometimes, doing the right thing isn't convenient. I could have played it safe, stayed in my lane, and left the hospital visit to someone else. But my conscience wouldn't let me.

I told my manager what I planned to do. I understood the risk—missing my flight, breaking protocol, facing consequences—but I was willing to carry that weight. This wasn't about protocol. It was about compassion.

I booked an Uber, asked the driver to wait for me, and rushed into the hospital's visitor area. When I finally reached Mr. Charles's room, he was awake and waiting. His eyes softened when he saw me.

He told me he had **Parkinson's disease** and confessed he'd recently considered ending his life. My heart sank.

I realized then how deeply alone he must have felt. And how much my presence—just showing up—had meant. I cried, overwhelmed by the gravity of his quiet pain. This wasn't just a detour from my day; it was a turning point in his.

Before leaving, I promised to help rebook his flight to Portland. Thankfully, I returned to the airport early enough to prepare for my next flight. The Uber driver and I shared a surprisingly deep conversation on the ride back—about humanity, compassion, and the quiet ways we can make a difference. He told me he admired the choice I made, even if it put my job at risk.

And I realized—I was glad I followed through. The anxiety of being late, the fear of crossing professional boundaries—all of it faded in comparison to the quiet, powerful impact of simply being there for someone in need.

That day, the hospital didn't discharge Mr. Charles. I spoke with his daughter in Portland and his brother in Burlington to inform them of his condition and whereabouts. They were relieved to hear from someone who had seen him, someone who cared. Over the following days, I learned more about Mr. Charles—his life, his family, his challenges. The more I understood, the more determined I became to follow through on my promise.

By then, I had flown to Budapest, Hungary, on a Holy Week personal mission. Even across an ocean, I stayed in contact with him and his family, helping to reschedule his ticket—twice. A few days later, Mr. Charles was finally discharged. He made it to Portland.

Not long after, I received a message from him: *"Thank you. I am trying to emulate your selfless actions. My sister would like to thank you as well."* It was simple, but deeply sincere. And that sincerity stayed with me.

We kept in touch for a while after. I knew he needed someone to talk to, and I was glad to be that person, even briefly. Our bond — formed in the unlikeliest of places — was proof that lives intersect for reasons we don't always understand in the moment.

Since then, I've often thought about Mr. Charles. About the courage it must have taken for him to travel alone with Parkinson's. About the private battles people fight while the world rushes by, unaware. And about how sometimes, the most life-changing actions aren't grand gestures, but quiet, deliberate choices to *show up*.

I've become more attuned since then — more aware of subtle signs in the passengers I serve and the people I pass by. A shaking hand. A look in someone's eyes. A slowness in movement. A silence that speaks volumes. I've started asking more often: *"Are you okay?"*

Because now, I understand the cost of walking past someone who isn't. Mr. Charles reminded me that compassion isn't always easy. It may involve discomfort, risk, or crossing into the unexpected. But it's worth it. It's *necessary*. And in a world that can often feel transactional or indifferent, it's these moments of humanity — raw, inconvenient, unpolished — that matter most.

The truth is, I almost missed this opportunity. But I didn't. I listened to my instincts. And for that, I'm grateful. Our captain's words echo in my mind still:"*Some individuals endure their struggles quietly.*" It's a simple statement, but it carries immense weight. Because it's true. Those individuals could be our passengers, our colleagues, family members, strangers at an airport gate — or even us.

So now, I carry Mr. Charles's story with me. A story of quiet courage, of silent suffering, and of the power of simply caring enough to pause. He was once a stranger. Now, he is someone who changed the way I see the world.

MISSION TRIP

There's something special about stepping outside your comfort zone to help others; it not only changes those you assist but also transforms you. The anticipation of these experiences fosters a strong sense of purpose. Whether building homes, teaching children, or donating to a worthy cause, each act of kindness leaves a lasting impact on both the giver and the recipient.

I recall a memorable flight involving a group of passengers from a church returning from a mission trip in the Dominican Republic. They were all dressed in their organization's uniforms, and the joy on their faces was incredible. Their energy was truly infectious, filling the cabin with a positive vibe that was hard to ignore. Being around them filled me with motivation, and I couldn't help but feel inspired by their kindness and generosity.

As the plane soared above the clouds, laughter and stories filled the cabin, woven with a shared sense of achievement and camaraderie among the group. Their conversations painted vivid pictures of days spent working side by side, united by a purpose much greater than themselves. I was struck by the depth of their experiences, which went beyond the projects they finished. They shared lessons in humility, gratitude, and the importance of teamwork, highlighting the transformative power of service.

In their presence, I saw the absolute truth that every mission, whether big or small, sends out ripples, touching lives in unseen ways. Their journey wasn't just about reaching a destination but about following their hearts' path, each guided by acts of service. The connections formed go beyond language and culture, transforming brief meetings into meaningful bonds.

I've known for a long time that service isn't a one-way street. Just as I give, I also receive. A mission trip is both humble and empowering, showing me that true service depends not on how far you travel but on how much you care. Whenever I see mission groups at the airport or during our flights, it reminds me that helping others creates a ripple effect, inspiring more people and strengthening my desire to serve wherever I am needed.

Being around mission volunteers reminds me that service is an ongoing journey. Every act of compassion builds bridges — between people, cultures, and most importantly, within ourselves. Travel shouldn't be limited to leisure; it can also serve as a platform for mission trips, making our journeys more meaningful. Seize every opportunity to make a positive impact wherever you go. My advocacy: Travel and Inspire. This philosophy resonates deeply with me, and I hope to share it with others through my stories and experiences.

♥

MS. LITTLE CHAMPION

One of the most memorable experiences of being a flight attendant is meeting extraordinary people who embody the spirit of a champion. Recently, I had the privilege of meeting a young girl who traveled all the way to the U.S. to compete in a tennis tournament. At just ten years old, she radiates a presence that belies her age: bright eyes full of determination, a shy but confident smile, and hands that grip a tennis racquet with the steadiness of someone far beyond her years. She is not just representing her country; she is carrying the dreams and pride of everyone cheering her on from home.

Accompanied by her father and sister, she carefully clutches a large tennis ball covered in signatures—a tangible reminder of her journey and the countless people who have supported her. The ball seems almost too big for her small hands, yet she holds it with reverence, as if cradling a treasure. Her movements on and off the court are precise and graceful, reflecting hours of practice and a mind focused on continual improvement. She is more than just a rising star; she is a testament to what passion and discipline can achieve.

Victory alone does not define a champion; it is the spirit and mindset with which they face each challenge. A true champion overcomes obstacles with perseverance and a strong sense of purpose. They strive for excellence not only in their achievements but also in their attitude—seeing setbacks as opportunities to grow, finding strength in adversity, and pushing forward when the going gets tough. The air of determination around them is almost tangible, visible in the way they carry themselves, the intensity in their eyes, and the quiet confidence in their movements.

A champion's mindset, like hers, is shaped not just by triumphs but also by trials. Every fall teaches resilience, every small victory fuels motivation, and every challenge becomes a stepping stone toward growth. I could see it in her posture, the way she bounces lightly on the balls of her feet, ready to spring into action at any moment, and in the quiet intensity of her gaze as she watched others practice around her. This inner strength, invisible to some but unmistakable to those who look closely, drives champions to pursue their dreams relentlessly while inspiring others to aim higher and dream bigger.

Some people are born with natural talent, while others discover it through practice, dedication, and perseverance. For this girl, talent and hard work intersect seamlessly. Even at such a young age, she experiences moments of doubt and self-discovery—moments that test her resolve and reveal hidden layers of strength. Each match she plays, each serve she perfects, and each challenge she overcomes builds her character, preparing her for both victories and setbacks alike.

What truly distinguishes a champion, however, is their mindset. It is a unique blend of resilience, humility, and unwavering optimism. Their focus extends beyond trophies or accolades, centering instead on consistent self-improvement, belief in their potential, and the courage to continue when others might falter. This young girl embodies these qualities fully, and in watching her, one cannot help but feel inspired. Her story is a reminder that greatness is not limited by age, experience, or circumstance — it is sparked by passion, nurtured through perseverance, and defined by the mindset that refuses to give up.

ONE STEP AT A TIME

Every day at work brings new faces, new stories, and fleeting moments that sometimes leave a lasting mark. Occasionally, someone boards the plane whose presence stills the cabin, commands my full attention, and humbles me with the quiet weight of their history.

One of those rare passengers was Dora Zaidenweber — a remarkable woman, a Holocaust survivor, and one of the most unforgettable people I have ever met. She boarded the flight to Minneapolis, Minnesota, alone, leaning on a cane, her movements slow and deliberate. Each step she took felt intentional, as though she had been taking careful steps all her life.

As I welcomed her aboard, I sensed she carried not just a bag, but decades of memory. There was something about her presence — an unspoken gravity — that made me slow down, watch, and really see her. I helped her find her seat, gently stowed her bag, and she looked at me with kind, grateful eyes. "Thank you," she said softly.

When the other passengers had settled, Dora gazed quietly out the window. The bustling cabin noise seemed to fade around her. There was dignity in the way she sat, a quiet grace that commanded respect.

Midway through the flight, Dora needed to use the restroom. She took my hand, and together we walked slowly, one careful step at a time. She was cheerful and lighthearted despite the effort it took to move through the aisle. I matched my pace to hers, aware that in this small act—guiding her hand, steadying her steps—I was participating in something meaningful. By the time we returned to her seat, I felt as though I had been granted the honor of accompanying living history.

After the flight, I couldn't stop thinking about Dora. Her presence lingered with me long after she had deplaned. I wanted to know more about her story.

According to the University of Minnesota:

"Zaidenweber, from Radom, Poland, was just 15 years old when Germany invaded her home country. And for the next six years, she lived under the shadow of death and uncertainty—from the Radom ghetto to Auschwitz and finally Bergen-Belsen—until that bright, sunny day in April when the British Army liberated the camp. Zaidenweber eventually reunited with her immediate family, and in 1950, they relocated to Minnesota. By the early '50s, they were among some 1,300 survivors of the Holocaust who resettled in the state following the war. Zaidenweber passed away last fall at age 99."

Learning this deepened my awe. I kept thinking about that short walk to the restroom—her hand in mine, her steps so deliberate. In that moment, I wasn't just helping a passenger. I was walking beside a woman who had endured horrors most of us can only read about, a woman who still carried herself with warmth and grace.

January 27 is International Holocaust Remembrance Day. Every year when it comes, I think of Dora—her quiet strength, her smile as we posed for a photo together, her reminder that resilience is not loud but steady.

Encounters like this one change you. They remind you that every passenger has a hidden story, that the people we meet on ordinary days may carry extraordinary histories. Dora taught me patience, compassion, and what it truly means to take life one step at a time.

PICTORIAL FLIGHT

T here's a unique energy that fills the air whenever people travel—a mix of anticipation and wonder that makes even the ordinary feel worth remembering. The airplane cabin transforms into a stage where smiles are shared, moments are frozen, and stories are quietly told through the click of a camera. The soft hum of the engines, the view of endless clouds outside, and the thought of a new destination often inspire passengers to reach for their phones, eager to capture proof of where they've been and how they felt in that fleeting moment.

On a recent flight to Buffalo, New York, I had the joy of meeting a group of women whose excitement was infectious. Two were tourists from China, their voices full of laughter as they filmed their walk down the aisle. The third, an artist from Russia, wore a bright scarf and an even brighter smile, chatting animatedly about their plan to visit Niagara Falls in Canada. Their enthusiasm lit up the cabin like sunshine spilling through the windows.

From the moment they boarded, they snapped pictures of everything— their seats, the plane, the view outside. I couldn't help but smile as I watched them, feeling their delight ripple through the cabin. It reminded me of my first few flights, when every detail felt new and worth remembering.

When we landed in Buffalo, the women didn't rush to leave. Instead, they turned to me with an almost childlike eagerness: "Photo? With you?" one asked, her phone already in hand. Their joy was so contagious that I didn't hesitate—I jumped right in.

We posed together in the narrow aisle, laughing as we tried to fit everyone into the frame. One of the women hugged me so tightly that it felt as if we'd known each other for years instead of a single flight. The shutter clicked over and over, capturing more than just smiles—it captured a moment of connection.

As a flight attendant, I meet hundreds of passengers every week, but there was something about these women that stayed with me. They reminded me that photos aren't just for social media—they are little keepsakes of joy, proof that for a few hours, strangers from across the globe shared the same sky, the same space, and the same happiness.

Not everyone would enjoy being the center of attention like that, and that's okay. Some of us prefer quiet interactions over enthusiastic photo sessions. But in this moment, I was glad to be part of their joy.

As they walked off the plane, waving and still giggling, I realized that encounters like these are what make travel magical. For a brief moment, language barriers and cultural differences disappeared. All that remained was the universal language of laughter, a reminder that we are more alike than we are different.

Making someone smile is one of the simplest, most powerful gifts we can give. On that day, those women reminded me that the best souvenirs we carry home from our travels aren't always tucked into a bag—they live in our hearts, preserved in shared moments, one picture at a time.

SERVING MR. CONGRESSMAN

Every flight feels like a stage play with a rotating cast of characters—business travelers with furrowed brows, vacationers buzzing with excitement, seasoned jetsetters with their routines perfected, and the occasional VIP whose very presence shifts the atmosphere. No two flights are ever the same, and no matter how many miles we log, we never quite know who will settle into those first-class seats or what silent expectations they'll bring aboard with them.

That morning, the plane was bathed in soft gold light as the sun climbed higher, streaming through the galley windows and casting long shadows on the floor. The day felt promising—calm air, a clear route, and a smooth flight ahead. I was paired with another new flight attendant, Rosie, someone just as eager and green as I was. Together, we started prepping the galley. We talked quietly as we set up the service cart, swapping stories about the challenges and small victories of our early days on the job. It was an easy, companionable rhythm—one that made the time pass quickly.

What we didn't realize was that our cheerful conversation had drifted forward, carried by the stillness of the cabin, into first class, where silence was part of the unspoken luxury.

When it was time for me to begin service in the first-class

cabin, the shift in energy was palpable. The air seemed heavier somehow, and the usual warm hum of anticipation was absent. I approached seat 2A with a practiced smile and asked the gentleman what he would like to drink.

He turned to me, his expression lined with irritation, and said, "You girls talk too much," his hand mimicking chatter with sharp precision.

The words hit me like a splash of cold water. My chest tightened with embarrassment, my professional smile freezing for half a beat before I quickly apologized. I explained that I'd been helping my colleague prepare the galley cart, but he didn't respond—just gave me a look, glanced deliberately at my name tag, and turned away.

I walked back to the galley, my thoughts churning. Had we been too loud? Too casual? Had we crossed some invisible line of first-class etiquette? For a moment, shame threatened to take over, whispering that I'd failed some test I hadn't even known I was taking. But I reminded myself that this was part of the job— learning, adjusting, growing. I couldn't undo the past few minutes, but I could control everything that came after.

For the rest of the flight, I became hyper-aware of every detail—my tone of voice, my movements, the way I placed each drink on the tray table. I moved with intention, allowing every small action to reset the mood. Even when I was met with cool indifference, I offered warm professionalism. Slowly, my embarrassment turned into determination.

As we began our descent, I felt a quiet pride in how I'd handled the remainder of the service. When the cabin door finally opened,

I offered one last apology to the passenger as he deplaned. He didn't respond, didn't even look at me. But as he stepped off the aircraft, I saw a member of the cleaning crew waiting for him. She greeted him with a hug and a bright smile, and the cleaning lady told me that he was a former congressman.

In that moment, the entire interaction clicked into place. I realized that his expectations, his need for quiet, and perhaps even his reaction had little to do with me personally. People carry their titles, their histories, and their moods with them wherever they go—and sometimes we happen to cross paths at the wrong moment.

That day taught me one of the most valuable lessons of my career: professionalism isn't about being perfect, it's about being grounded enough to stay calm, adapt, and carry yourself with grace even when things don't go your way. I can't control another person's attitude, but I can control my own. I can choose to meet rudeness with dignity, criticism with humility, and frustration with patience.

Being new gave me that chance to learn. That uncomfortable exchange became a quiet milestone—proof that every difficult encounter has the potential to shape us for the better. The cabin may have felt tense that day, but it left me feeling more assertive, more self-aware, and more committed to meeting every passenger, no matter their status or mood, with the same steady professionalism.

♥

STOLEN KISS

Some moments in life shine with innocence and spontaneity, creating memories that linger long after the day ends. These are the moments that don't require photographs to be remembered—they're etched in the heart, carried quietly, a gentle reminder of connection. Sometimes, they come in the form of genuine affection, sweet and unguarded, like a tender kiss offered in gratitude during a journey.

On a flight from Toronto, Canada, to New York City, I met a little boy traveling with his mother. For him, airplanes were a distant marvel, glimpsed only in books, movies, or brief mentions. Stepping into the airport for the first time, he was wide-eyed with wonder, each sight and sound new, exciting, and a little overwhelming.

I told him a little secret: when we landed, he'd get to see the pilot up close. The excitement in his eyes was immediate and radiant, a beam of pure delight that made the entire cabin feel warmer. Each moment of the flight seemed to heighten his anticipation—he pressed his face against the window, marveling at the clouds, fascinated by the hum of engines, and eagerly soaking in every detail of this airborne adventure.

When the time came for him to step onto the flight deck, I watched him with a smile. His small hands reached toward the controls in awe, his eyes sparkling as the pilot spoke, explaining the levers and lights. He was mesmerized by a world so different from his own—a tiny explorer discovering the secrets of the sky.

After the tour, I crouched down to his level and lifted him into a hug, sharing his joy. Then, in a spontaneous, heart-melting moment, he gave me a quick, shy stolen kiss. His mother captured it with a photograph, but even that image couldn't hold the quiet magic of the air between us in that instant. She looked at me, eyes glistening, and whispered her thanks, her pride and emotion palpable.

The stolen kiss wasn't just gratitude—it was wonder made visible, a gift from one heart to another, a fleeting connection that reminded me how travel is often less about places visited and more about moments shared. It was a tiny, perfect exchange of joy and human warmth.

As the boy and his mother walked away, I silently hoped this memory would linger for him, too. Perhaps one day, he would recall the thrill of his first flight and the magic of a stolen kiss, and let it inspire dreams as limitless as the skies he had just touched.

Looking back, I realized that the true magic of travel lies not only in discovering new lands but also in forging unexpected connections. These moments of pure, simple affection—like a stolen kiss—remind us that to be seen and celebrated doesn't require grand gestures, only the sharing of our genuine spirit.

♥

THANK YOU FOR YOUR SERVICE, SIR

E very veteran's story is a living testament to resilience and honor. Their lives remind us that freedom is never an accident, never free, and never without cost. It is safeguarded by men and women who stood ready to face danger, to endure hardship, and to sacrifice for a cause greater than themselves. Through their courage and unwavering devotion to liberty and democracy, they etched a legacy that time cannot erase. These legacies are not just written in history books — they live in the hearts and memories of those who carry them forward.

My years with the U.S. Department of Veterans Affairs in the Philippines gave me a front-row seat to that legacy. Serving veterans and their families taught me that service does not end when the uniform is set aside. It continues in the lives they touch, in the values they uphold, and in the resilience they embody. That experience instilled something deep within me: a sense of obligation to honor veterans whenever I cross paths with them. Whether in my personal life or at work, I try never to miss the chance to look them in the eye and say, "Thank you for your service." A simple phrase, but one that carries the weight of immeasurable gratitude.

One flight from JFK to Tampa, Florida, became more than just another journey in the sky — it became a moment of history. It was our honor to welcome Mr. Farden, a World War II veteran, on board. To meet him was to step into the presence of living history, to shake hands with a man who helped shape the freedoms we enjoy today. He carried himself with quiet dignity, the kind that does not demand attention yet commands respect. His eyes spoke volumes — stories of hardship and hope, of battles fought and friends lost, of freedom preserved at great cost.

What moved me most was his humility. Despite his role in a defining moment of world history, Mr. Farden never boasted. He did not frame his actions in terms of heroism or glory. For him, it was a duty. Service was simply what had to be done. That kind of humility is rare and humbling to witness. It shifts your perspective, reminding you that the greatest acts of courage often come from those who never sought recognition.

The cabin filled with quiet reverence as passengers realized who we had on board. Some offered handshakes, others offered applause, and many simply watched with a mix of gratitude and awe. Welcoming him wasn't just a formal gesture — it was an act of remembrance. For me personally, taking a photo with him was more than a keepsake. It was a way of saying that this encounter mattered, that his life and service left an imprint on all of us who shared that flight.

In honoring our veterans, we do more than pay tribute to the past — we reaffirm the values that unite us in the present. Their sacrifices echo in every privilege we enjoy, reminding us that our freedoms are tied to their willingness to stand in harm's way. A handshake, a whispered thank you, a moment of applause may seem small, yet they carry immense weight. These gestures are more than politeness; they are acts of connection, acknowledgments that their stories continue to shape who we are as a people.

Each time we encounter a veteran, we stand before living history. These men and women are walking reminders of resilience, sacrifice, and community. Recognizing their contributions strengthens the fabric of our nation. It keeps alive the lessons of courage, duty, and service for future generations. Veterans like Mr. Farden are not only links to our past but also guiding lights for our future. They remind us that while battles may be fought on foreign soil, the true legacy of service is written in the lives of those who come after.

Every encounter with a veteran is an opportunity. An opportunity to express gratitude, to honor sacrifice, and to carry forward the values they defended. Through grand gestures and humble words alike, we keep their stories alive. By thanking them, by remembering them, by telling their stories, we ensure that their sacrifices never fade into silence.

So, to Mr. Farden, and to every veteran who has carried the weight of service: thank you. Thank you for your courage, your endurance, and your example. Your legacy lives not only in history but in the hearts of all who remember.

♥

JUST ONE SMILE

There is a quiet magic in the simple act of turning up the corners of your lips. A smile, especially when genuine, carries a power we often underestimate. It can break through language barriers, soften a hardened mood, and offer a flicker of warmth in an otherwise chaotic world.

On one flight, as passengers began to gather their belongings and file toward the exit, a woman pressed a folded napkin into my hand. She gave a slight nod before stepping into the aisle. When the cabin finally emptied, I opened the napkin and read her message: *"Just one smile can transform someone's day. Enjoy your day. Safe flight."*

Her words stopped me. I smiled instinctively, realizing that the simple gesture I had offered her—a smile in passing—had meant more than I could have guessed. I wondered about her story. Was she grieving someone she loved? Did she carry worries about illness, or the weight of stress and exhaustion? I didn't know her circumstances, yet I knew that, for a brief moment, my smile had made her day a little lighter.

That napkin became more than just a scrap of paper. It was proof that the smallest actions ripple outward, often reaching farther than we can see. I slipped it into my pocket, determined to keep it close. Every time I felt tired or drained, I could pull it out and remember: kindness matters. A smile matters.

Flying places us in contact with so many lives, each passenger carrying unseen stories. Some greet us with laughter and conversation. Others stay quiet, watching from their seats, taking in every detail. Not everyone speaks their truth out loud, yet they still notice the energy we bring—the tone of our voice, the patience in our responses, and yes, the sincerity of our smiles.

That napkin reminded me that gratitude and kindness flow both ways. I had given her a smile, and she returned it to me in words I could hold in my hands. To her, it was likely a small gesture. To me, it was a treasure.

I know how hard it is to smile when you are exhausted, sick, overwhelmed, or weighed down by sadness. On those days, a smile feels impossible. And yet, when we choose to smile anyway, we shift something inside ourselves. It does not erase the hardship, but it softens the edges. It allows light to slip in.

At 35,000 feet, among strangers heading in a thousand different directions, a smile becomes more than an expression—it becomes a bridge. A small bond forms, invisible but real, reminding us that even in our separateness, we share a common sky.

That one napkin, and the simple note written on it, reaffirmed something I already believed but often forget: kindness never disappears. It circles back. It connects us. It carries forward. And sometimes, all it takes to start that chain reaction is just one smile.

♥

AN UNPREDICTABLE JOURNEY:
NO GUARANTEE

I view my career as a flight attendant as a remarkable chapter in my life's ongoing story. Each flight is more than a commute — it's a microcosm of life itself, full of its own joys, challenges, surprises, and fleeting goodbyes. As the years pass and experience deepens, my perspective evolves. Colleagues become like family — not by blood, but through shared duties, trust, and countless hours spent navigating the skies together.

The airline industry thrives on unpredictability. Even a quick flight can turn chaotic — medical emergencies, weather delays, mechanical issues, or missed connections can transform a routine journey in minutes. Layovers are shortened, days off denied, and schedules shifted without warning. Every crew member learns quickly to adapt, stay calm, and focus on what can be controlled. In aviation, nothing is certain; everything is subject to the whims of wind, weather, and circumstance.

Life mirrors this unpredictability. Just as a flight's departure can never be guaranteed, neither is our time here on earth.

Among the many faces I've met above the clouds, one stands out vividly: a young, ambitious pilot whose dreams were as vast as the sky itself. We flew together often, sharing early-morning briefings, late-night arrivals, and quiet moments in the crew lounge. Our bond grew beyond mere professional courtesy. He confided in me about his family, his pressures, and the dreams driving him forward. In those moments, I became a surrogate mother of sorts, listening, offering guidance, and encouraging him to pursue his ambitions with courage.

His dedication was inspiring. With perseverance, he earned the title of captain, commanding larger aircraft and achieving the career milestone he had long worked for. Watching his success filled me with pride, as if his victories were my own. He embodied grace and humility in uniform, managing responsibilities with both competence and heart.

And then, as life often reminds us, joy and sorrow collide without warning. One evening, scrolling through Facebook, the world shifted. A post appeared—abrupt and stark: he had passed away unexpectedly. The shock was profound. Gone, just as he had begun the chapter he had long awaited. The grief settled deep in my chest, reminding me that life is fragile and fleeting. Our final conversation replayed in my mind, now heavy with the weight of permanence I had never anticipated.

It happens again and again in our profession. A flight attendant full of energy, kindness, and laughter is suddenly remembered in a memorial post. A pilot with dreams of captaincy has life cut short. A beloved colleague enjoys retirement for only a brief time before leaving us unexpectedly. These losses pierce through the illusion of permanence we cling to in daily life.

Such tragedies shift my perspective. I become more intentional, valuing every layover, every sunrise, and sunset above the clouds, every shared laugh in the galley. Knowing that every "goodbye" could be my last, I strive to make every "hello" meaningful.

The lessons are clear: embrace life's unpredictability. Don't wait for the perfect moment—create it. Pursue passions with urgency. Nurture relationships. Express love and gratitude openly and often. Travel to the destinations you dream of. Write the story waiting inside you. Share your light.

I honor those who have been lost by living fully, cherishing bonds that give this fleeting life meaning. Between flights, I reflect on the lessons learned at 35,000 feet, jotting them down in my journal, committed to telling stories that matter. Life isn't guaranteed.

Live intentionally. Love boldly. Be kind without reservation. Chase your dreams with courage. The runway is open, the sky is waiting—and every moment you take to soar is a gift.

THE EYES OF LOVE

L ove often speaks in silence. A glance. A smile. A touch that needs no explanation. Between two people who have weathered life's storms together, these small gestures become the truest language of devotion.

On a recent flight to JFK, I met a couple I will never forget. I call them Mr. and Mrs. Love. They were heading back to Africa, carrying with them a bond that felt both ordinary and extraordinary. Watching them, I didn't just see affection. I saw a living testimony to love's endurance.

Mr. Love sat in a wheelchair, unable to comply with our request to look at the camera. His eyes, however, never strayed from his wife. He watched her as if she were the only person in the room, his admiration quiet but unshakable. Mrs. Love met his gaze with a smile so radiant that it seemed to light the path before them. Their exchange said more than words could capture: a lifetime of promises kept, burdens carried together, joys shared side by side.

In that moment, I realized their love had been forged not in dramatic declarations but in the countless, ordinary days of choosing each other. Love, I saw, is not a single act but a daily decision — woven into gestures so subtle they might be missed by anyone who isn't paying attention.

When we parted ways at the jetbridge, the memory lingered. I carried with me a deeper understanding: true love reveals itself not in grand displays but in everyday devotion, in patience, in kindness, in steadfast presence.

Later, as I looked at the photo we took together, I thought of Melissa Manchester's song, *Looking Through the Eyes of Love*. The lyrics echoed their story. Now, every time I hear that song, I see Mr. and Mrs. Love, hand in hand, their bond unbroken, their eyes still fixed on each other.

Their love reminds me of something rare. A love that, no matter the distance, always finds its way home.

THREAT SYNDROME

The phrase struck me the first time I heard it: *threat syndrome*. At that moment, I had no context. I didn't know what it meant, and I certainly didn't know how it shaped the daily life of the woman sitting in front of me. But as the flight went on, I began to notice what the phrase was trying to explain. Her story was not told in words. It was written across her anxious glances, the small, sudden movements, the nervous energy she carried in her body.

I often wonder how many times we misread these signs in others. We see someone fidget, we see them restless, we notice discomfort, and we quickly label it as impatience or unease. Rarely do we stop to consider that those movements might carry a deeper story—a story of resilience, of coping, of living with something that cannot always be controlled.

She was a middle-aged woman traveling alone. What caught my attention first was the small pink stuffed toy she held close. At first glance, it seemed unusual. Stuffed toys are common on flights, but usually in the hands of children. In her hands, it felt different. It seemed to carry a weight, a purpose. She clutched it with the kind of care one gives to something that provides safety.

As the plane prepared for takeoff, I noticed her shifting uneasily in her seat. The movements were subtle but continuous. I sensed she wasn't comfortable, so I arranged for her to move to another seat where no one would be beside her. It was a small adjustment, but I hoped it would bring her some ease.

Later, she opened up to me. In a quiet voice, she said she had "threat syndrome." The words hung in the air. I didn't know what to make of them, but I could tell it took courage for her to admit it.

After the flight, I researched and discovered what she meant. The medical term was *Tourette syndrome*. The Mayo Clinic describes it as a neurological disorder that involves repetitive, involuntary movements or unwanted sounds called tics. These can include eye blinking, head jerking, shoulder shrugging, sniffing, throat clearing, grunting, repeating phrases, or even mimicking what others do or say. The exact cause is unknown, but studies suggest it arises from a mix of genetics and environment.

When I read that description, my mind went back to her pink stuffed toy. It was no longer just an accessory or a sentimental object. It was her shield. It was the anchor she carried to manage her condition and to feel secure in the unpredictable world outside herself. Where others might see weakness, I saw bravery. Traveling alone, carrying her burden, and trusting a stranger enough to share her reality—these were not signs of fragility. They were proof of a quiet, resilient strength.

As I reflected, I realized that vulnerability is so often mistaken for weakness. Yet in truth, it is one of the purest forms of courage. Her toy was more than fabric and stuffing. It was a reminder that we all reach for something to steady us. For some, it's faith. For others, it's relationships. For her, it was the comfort of holding that small figure as the world moved unpredictably around her.

The flight continued, and I found myself watching her with respect. I thought about how many people sit beside us every day, carrying invisible challenges. Some we notice. Others remain hidden. We rarely think about the strength required to step out into the world with those burdens, to sit on a crowded plane, to push forward despite the difficulty.

As the plane rose above the clouds, I reflected on the truth that every person has a story we do not see. Some of us meet those stories with kindness, while others respond with judgment or indifference. Compassion doesn't always require grand actions. Often, it is something small. It is giving someone space. It is recognizing their humanity without labeling or mocking. It is allowing them to exist as they are, without trying to explain them away.

When we landed and walked through the busy airport, the memory stayed with me. Crowds of people rushed past, each traveler focused on their own destination. Yet within that crowd, countless hidden struggles were being carried—some in silence, some with visible signs, some masked behind forced smiles. She reminded me that the only way to truly understand people is to pay attention, not just to what they say but to the silences between their words.

By the end of my workday, her image was still vivid in my mind. I thought again of the toy she clutched, of her openness, of her courage. And I realized something simple but profound: in a fast-moving world, the greatest gift we can offer is patience. To slow down. To look closer. To resist judgment. To give others the grace to handle their burdens in their own way.

That woman taught me a lesson she didn't even know she was teaching. She showed me that love and compassion are not always loud or dramatic. Sometimes they are quiet, almost invisible, but no less powerful. Sometimes they look like a pink stuffed toy, tightly held in the hands of someone traveling alone.

WE ARE DESCENDING!

C alm is not the absence of fear. It is the mastery of it. On an airplane, where emergencies can unfold in the blink of an eye, calm becomes both shield and lifeline. These moments reveal the best in people: the steady professionalism of the crew, the empathy passengers extend to one another, and the resilience that rises when strangers face uncertainty together.

That morning began like any other flight. Safety checks, briefings, and cheerful greetings flowed with the rhythm of routine. The cabin carried the gentle hum of conversation, the clatter of carry-ons, and the anticipation of another journey above the clouds. With seventy-two passengers on board, including a non-revenue flight attendant and several children, the atmosphere was expectant but light. I recall one mother, traveling with her two young sons for the very first time, her face lit with both excitement and nervousness. Everything about the day suggested normalcy.

The illusion of safety, however, is fragile. By late morning, that sense of ease gave way to something far less certain. We had closed the main cabin door around 11 AM. The flight unfolded smoothly at first. Agnes, my fellow flight attendant, had begun serving snacks, and I was busy taking orders from first-class passengers. Then she noticed something I had overlooked: we were descending. Immediately, she alerted me. I looked out the window and felt a knot in my stomach tighten — we were dropping.

I immediately reached for the interphone and called the cockpit. Silence. I tried again. Still no response. A wave of worry rose in me, knocking firmly on the cockpit door, my heart racing with possibilities I dared not voice. Were the pilots incapacitated? Was this descent uncontrolled? On the third attempt, the captain finally responded, his voice calm, measured, reassuring. Relief washed through me in an instant. He explained the situation: a pressurization issue required an immediate descent. He assured us it was under control. The landing would be normal, but we would divert to Philadelphia, Pennsylvania.

Even with the explanation, the tension in the cabin shifted dramatically. From the moment we began descending, the temperature inside rose. Airflow ceased, and the cabin quickly turned stifling — hot, humid, uncomfortable. Children began crying. Some passengers clutched their ears, wincing from the pressure. I felt the weight of dozens of anxious eyes on us, searching for reassurance.

The captain made his announcement, steady and calm, and I followed with my own. The words mattered less than the tone — measured, composed, grounded. In that heat, with emotions rising, passengers needed to feel steadiness more than anything else. Agnes and I moved through the cabin, securing belongings, answering questions, and offering comfort where we could. One mother whispered fears about her two sons, her hand trembling slightly as she held theirs.

The non-revenue flight attendant stepped in quietly, lending extra support. Small acts of teamwork made a heavy burden lighter.

We landed safely in Philadelphia at 12:20 PM. The descent, though tense, had been handled with skill and precision by the pilots. On the ground, supervisors met us, and we were told another plane would arrive from Detroit at 3:15 PM. The next few hours blurred into a mixture of reassurance and waiting. The gate area buzzed with conversation—questions, concerns, fatigue. By the time the replacement aircraft arrived, a collective sigh of relief swept through everyone, like a wave releasing its tension. Boarding again, this time with more smiles than frowns, felt like a small victory. At 3:35 PM, we departed with every passenger accounted for.

When we touched down in Charlotte, North Carolina at 4:10 PM, gratitude poured forth. Passengers thanked us as they deplaned, some offering words of encouragement, others simply saying, "Thank you for keeping us safe." Many complimented our calm, our teamwork, our reassurance. I made sure to thank Agnes for being such a steady partner, and I commended the pilots for their swift actions that prevented decompression.

As a new flight attendant, I questioned myself in the quiet moments afterward. Did I do enough? Did my nerves show? Could I have been steadier? But alongside those doubts was pride—pride in the teamwork that carried us through, pride in Agnes's composure, pride in the way we collectively faced the unknown.

When the last passenger walked down the jetbridge, and the cabin finally quieted, Agnes and I shared a brief look—an unspoken acknowledgment of what we had just experienced. Emergencies have a way of forging silent bonds. Words were unnecessary. We understood each other in that glance.

The day that had promised a quick flight and an afternoon trip to a lighthouse ended instead with weary bodies resting by the pool, recovering from adrenaline and stress. Plans shifted, but perspective deepened.

That night, in my hotel room, fatigue mixed with gratitude. I thought about the passengers who had trusted us, about the mother who calmed her sons, about the stranger who lent a hand, and about the pilots who guided us down safely. I realized once more what this job truly means. A flight attendant isn't just someone who serves food and drink. We are guardians of safety, stewards of calm, and keepers of compassion.

The unpredictability of flight mirrors life itself. Turbulence is inevitable. Emergencies are never scheduled. But within those moments, grace can rise—grace shown through teamwork, resilience, and human connection. And as I closed my eyes that night, one truth remained clear: flying is not just about reaching a destination. It is about traveling together, with courage, patience, and compassion, even through the unexpected descents along the way.

♥

WINTER HAT

There is a special warmth in giving away something you love. True giving isn't about sacrifice or loss. It's about sharing a part of yourself — offering comfort, hope, or a quiet reminder that someone cares. When you stop measuring an object by its personal value and instead see the relief it can bring to another person, the act becomes extraordinary. The real treasure isn't the object at all. It is the kindness that travels with it.

That truth came alive for me on a cold, rainy morning as we prepared for our flight to Raleigh-Durham, North Carolina. The wind was sharp, the kind that bites through clothing and lingers on your skin. Everyone hurried about their duties, heads down, shoulders hunched against the weather. Amid that scene, I noticed Star, the catering lady, working on our flight. She moved quickly, loading supplies, her hair damp from the drizzle. What struck me was that she wasn't wearing a hat.

It was a simple observation, but it lingered. I felt a small tug inside, the kind of quiet nudge that often comes before an unexpected act of kindness. Without overthinking, I walked up to her and asked, "Do you want my hat?"

Her response was immediate. She smiled and said yes, no hesitation, no polite decline. I went to my luggage, pulled out my favorite winter hat, and handed it to her. She slipped it on, and in that instant her entire face lit up. Her eyes shone with gratitude.

Her smile was wide and genuine. It was such a small gesture, yet it created a moment where the cold seemed to fade. We even paused to take a couple of selfies, capturing the quiet joy of that exchange.

Watching Star work that morning, I realized kindness often begins with noticing. Too often, we are so caught up in our own duties and distractions that we miss the needs of those right in front of us. Yet, in seeing her discomfort, an opportunity appeared. I could replace a hat. But I couldn't replace the chance to share warmth in that exact moment.

The hat, once mine, had found a new purpose. It no longer served only to keep me warm; it had become a gift, bringing her comfort and filling my own heart with joy. I walked away, reminded that every encounter holds an invitation to do good. We may never know the full impact of our small actions. Perhaps that hat was only a token. But perhaps, on a cold and tiring day, it carried hope.

Giving is never one-sided. When we give, we also receive— sometimes more than we expect. A simple gesture becomes a thread, weaving two lives together for a brief moment in time, reminding us that humanity is strongest when it is shared.

Later, as I wrapped up my day in the lingering winter chill, I reflected on my everyday mantra: *help someone today*. I smiled, knowing I had lived it out. The weather remained cold, but inside, I felt only warmth. Because warmth, once shared, is never truly lost.

♥

A SHARED DREAM

Dreams are powerful. They are more than private hopes hidden away in our hearts. They shape who we become, push us forward when life feels uncertain, and give us reasons to keep moving. Often, we meet people whose dreams echo our own. In them, we see the reflection of our past, and in their stories, we find reminders of how important it is to encourage others along the way.

One early morning in Virginia, I met a young Filipina working at the hotel. She greeted me with a shy smile, her quiet warmth shining through her reserved demeanor. Our conversation began lightly, touching on our homeland and her family. Then she revealed something personal: her dream of becoming a flight attendant. She spoke softly, almost cautiously, as though sharing something very close to her heart. Yet in her eyes, I caught a glimpse of determination.

Her words stirred me. I remembered my own early days when I, too, stood in her shoes, dreaming of the skies, filled with ambition but unsure of how or when doors would open. That memory made me lean in with genuine interest. I began to share advice from my own journey—how confidence and communication matter, how rejection is never final, and how preparation often makes the difference when opportunity finally arrives. I encouraged her to stay motivated, to keep learning, and to believe that her dream was within reach.

Her expression shifted as she listened, and I could see hope growing stronger in her. What might have seemed like a casual conversation became, for both of us, something more meaningful. For me, it was a reminder that helping others carries a unique joy. Encouragement is never wasted—it's like watering a seed. Sometimes a single kind word is enough to keep a dream alive.

As I walked away, I thought about how success is not measured only by personal achievements but also by the impact we leave behind. Our lives are made richer when we use our experiences to inspire others, to pass on the lessons we've learned, and to remind someone that their dream is worth chasing.

That young woman may not remember every word I said, but I hope she remembers how she felt—that someone believed in her. And I will remember her too, because she reminded me of a truth I carry with me: every dream matters, and sometimes all it takes is encouragement from another traveler on the journey.

A HUG

T here are moments in life when the simplest gestures carry the deepest meaning. A hug, unplanned and unpretentious, has the power to express what words cannot. It can bridge the gap between strangers, turn sorrow into comfort, and remind us that kindness still has the strength to heal.

Breakfast has always been an important ritual for me, especially during long layovers. At one of my favorite New York hotels, I often enjoy their buffet in the calm of the morning before the day takes its pace. On this particular morning, while savoring my meal, I noticed a quiet tension across the dining area. A young staff member sat with someone who appeared to be her supervisor. Their conversation was serious. I couldn't hear their words, but I saw her wiping away tears, her posture heavy, her face clouded by worry.

I wondered what her story was. Was she being reprimanded? Was she dealing with something heavy in her personal life? I didn't know, but the sight of her tears lingered in my thoughts as I finished my breakfast.

As the two women stood to leave, I felt an inner nudge. Something simple but strong urged me to approach. Walking up to the young woman, I gently asked, "Can I hug you? You'll be fine. Things will get better." She looked at me with tired eyes, then smiled softly and said, "Thank you." Her supervisor quickly added, "She's okay," as if to reassure me. But I had already seen enough to know she needed that moment.

That small exchange stayed with me. It reminded me of how important social awareness is—the ability to notice, to pause, and to respond with empathy. Often, people don't need grand solutions. Sometimes all they need is acknowledgment, a kind word, or a gentle gesture to remind them they are not invisible.

As flight attendants, social awareness is a skill we must carry everywhere. It helps us connect with passengers, sense unspoken needs, and offer more than just service—we offer human connection. But beyond the cabin, it matters in every part of life. To notice. To listen. To care.

I was a stranger to her, yet that hug created a shared moment of humanity. For just a brief instant, she smiled through her sadness. And in that moment, I was reminded that compassion doesn't require permission or familiarity—only presence and sincerity.

♥

BEYOND LANGUAGE

Effective communication is more than words. It is empathy — our ability to feel another person's emotions and respond with understanding — that allows us to truly connect and offer support.

One day during boarding, I was alerted about a passenger in distress. She was an elderly woman who spoke no English. She was upset, crying, and hesitant to step onto the aircraft. She spoke rapidly in her native language, her voice filled with fear, though no one around her could understand. For a moment, the gate agent even considered denying her boarding because of her emotional state.

After a discussion among the crew, we agreed to let her board. Still, I knew we needed a way to ease her fear. I asked the gate agent to check her emergency contact information. We were able to reach her son by phone, and I explained the situation while she stood beside me. I then handed her the phone. The change was immediate. As soon as she heard her son's voice, the tears slowed, her body relaxed, and her expression softened. The fear that had consumed her seemed to lift.

When the flight took off, and we reached cruising altitude, I walked through the cabin to check on her. To my surprise, I found her speaking in English with her seatmate, smiling, and laughing as if the earlier distress had never happened. I smiled quietly to myself and didn't ask for any explanation. I didn't need one.

That experience showed me that language itself isn't the true barrier. The real barrier is a lack of empathy. Communication is about more than speaking the same words. It is about listening with patience, creating a safe environment, and showing compassion. Sometimes the most powerful connections are made without words—through a reassuring touch, a patient smile, or a calm presence.

What I learned is simple. Compassion is the universal language. It can calm fear, ease loneliness, and bring people together when words fail. In a world filled with diverse languages, cultures, and backgrounds, empathy reminds us of our shared humanity. And when we choose to practice it, we create a better experience not only for others but also for ourselves.

♥

CONGRATS TO THE BRIDE AND HER BEST FRIEND

Friendship is a rare treasure. It is a mirror that reflects our best selves and a steady light that guides us through the darkest times. To have a best friend is to experience a relationship built on encouragement, loyalty, honesty, and love.

On one particular flight, this truth came alive in the form of two women whose laughter carried down the aisle, impossible to ignore. Their joy was so contagious that even before I knew their story, I could feel their energy brighten the cabin.

We were flying out of Nashville, Tennessee—a city with its own reputation for music, hospitality, and celebration. Known as the country's music hub and one of the most popular destinations for bachelorette parties in the United States, Nashville offers its visitors vibrant nightlife, charm, and affordability. It was the perfect setting for what unfolded that day.

Seated together, two beautiful women had transformed their small corner of the aircraft into a joyful stage. The bride's best friend had carefully decorated the area with banners and elegant cups, a thoughtful surprise to mark the occasion. All that was missing was a sparkling toast to complete their airborne celebration.

"You're lucky to have such a supportive and creative friend. Congratulations!" I said warmly to the bride. With that, I offered them complimentary champagne. Their faces lit up as we clinked glasses and said, "Cheers!" The mood in the cabin shifted. Smiles spread across nearby passengers, the women's laughter floated softly through the air, and for a brief moment, strangers shared in their happiness.

When the bride and her best friend thanked me, their eyes sparkled with gratitude and anticipation for the journey ahead. Watching them reminded me that travel is never just about the destination. It is about the moments that surprise us, the connections we make, and the memories created along the way. With something as simple as friendship, laughter, and a shared toast, an ordinary flight became unforgettable.

SOMEONE IS
WATCHING ME

There's a particular vulnerability in being watched — an invisible invitation for someone to interpret your actions, your mood, your gestures, even your character.

As a flight attendant, I've grown used to the subtle glances from passengers. Some are curious, some quietly observant, and others are likely judging. It comes with the job: you are on display, whether you're energized and smiling or running on empty. Even when I'm tired, sad, or distracted, my role calls for professionalism. Sometimes I wonder what stories passengers create about me as I move down the aisle — what they notice, what they assume, what they remember once they leave the plane.

One day on a flight from Detroit to Rochester, New York, I was running on fumes. My body felt sluggish, my eyelids heavy. I kept reminding myself to stay present: passengers notice everything, even when you're running low on energy. The flight was short, routine, and quiet, the kind of leg where you count down the minutes until you can breathe for a moment.

When we landed, I stayed behind to chat with the gate agent about our next flight. "There's a passenger who wants to thank you," she said, nodding toward a man approaching.

I expected him to say he'd left something on the plane. Instead, he walked right up to me, looked me in the eye, and said, "You are so compassionate. I've never seen somebody like you."

My tired brain defaulted to humor. "Oh, someone *was* watching me!" I joked, before thanking him sincerely.

"Yes," he said simply. "I was watching you do your job."

His words hit me harder than I expected. As I walked back through the jetbridge, I kept replaying the flight in my mind. What had he seen? Was it the way I helped the elderly couple find their seats? The patience in my tone when explaining something? The small, unnoticed gestures that I didn't think twice about?

Whatever it was, his compliment dissolved my fatigue. I felt lighter, brighter—reminded that even on my most exhausting days, my presence matters.

Each flight I work, I notice so many small, tender moments: a parent rocking a restless baby, a couple sharing a private laugh, lovers holding hands, a grown child guiding an elderly parent down the aisle. I've always thought of myself as the observer, collecting quiet stories from the cabin around me. But that day reminded me that I, too, am part of the story someone else is telling.

Sometimes life feels like a blur of flights and schedules, a long string of days when no one seems to notice the effort it takes to keep going. But every now and then, someone does notice. Someone is watching, quietly appreciating, and holding up a mirror that reflects the light you carry — even when you think you have none left.

DOWNSIZING

Downsizing is more than a trend—it's a mindset, a deliberate decision to strip away the excess and make room for what truly matters. The idea of owning less and living simply has always felt appealing to me. There's something freeing about traveling lighter, moving more quickly, and carrying only what you need. In theory, downsizing promises clarity and convenience. In practice, however, it sometimes comes with lessons you don't expect.

As a flight attendant, my luggage is practically an extension of my uniform. It travels everywhere with me, enduring long layovers, quick turnarounds, and endless miles. On a small 50-seater plane, space is limited, and stowing a fully packed suitcase for a four-day trip can feel like a puzzle every time. In an effort to make my life easier, I decided to downsize—to trade my standard luggage for a smaller, lighter, and admittedly cheaper one.

It wasn't a perfect luggage; the zipper caught a little too often—but I convinced myself it would work. Until, of course, it didn't. On the last morning of my trip in Cincinnati, Ohio, the zipper finally gave way. I stood there in the hotel room staring at my open suitcase, clothes threatening to spill everywhere. It was an embarrassing moment, but also one of those moments you just have to roll with. Thankfully, the hotel staff came to my rescue with some tape, and I managed to hold everything together long enough to finish the trip.

By the time I returned home, my battered little suitcase had become more than just broken luggage—it had become a lesson in adaptability, humility, and humor. I had to accept that my attempt to simplify had backfired and face the awkwardness of walking through the airport with taped-up luggage.

But here's the thing: the experience left me laughing. It reminded me that life's mishaps aren't just inconveniences—they're opportunities to grow, to learn, and sometimes, to smile at yourself. Downsizing can be freeing, but it only works when done intentionally and wisely. Not every shortcut leads to a smoother journey.

Sometimes, the most valuable souvenirs we bring home from our trips are the stories—the ones that humble us, teach us resilience, and give us something to laugh about later. And now, whenever I pack for a trip, I do so with a little more wisdom, a little better luggage, and a renewed appreciation for flexibility when things go wrong.

♥

A YOUNG GIRL'S DREAM

Sometimes, a dream begins quietly and early, nurtured by the gentle support of family. It only takes a kind word, a shared story, or a simple photograph to help a dreamer take flight.

I met Liz and her grandparents while waiting at the gate for our flight from Knoxville, Tennessee, to Daytona Beach, Florida. Her grandmother, with a warm and gentle demeanor, approached us and asked if we could take a photo with Liz. She explained that Liz has always admired flight attendants and dreams of becoming one someday. My colleague, Rissa, and I gladly posed, and Liz's excitement was written all over her face. She carried herself with the quiet grace of a well-mannered granddaughter, her southern charm shining through in her polite "thank you."

As the camera clicked, I couldn't help but wonder what that picture would mean to her in the years ahead. Would it be taped to her bedroom wall, tucked away in a scrapbook, or shown proudly to her friends as a reminder that her dream is possible? In that moment, I silently wished Liz courage, patience, and determination. Sometimes a small gesture, like a simple photograph, can become a powerful reminder that what we aspire to is within reach.

Everyone, like Liz, has dreams. Some take root early, ignited by childhood curiosity and nurtured by family encouragement. Others awaken later in life, born from unexpected turns or long-held desires finally allowed to grow. Both paths hold beauty.

I know this well because I became a flight attendant at 44. While some might see that as late, for me, it was perfect timing. The dream had been in my heart for years, quietly waiting, and when the opportunity came, it blossomed fully. Today, every flight feels like the harvest of seeds planted long ago—dreams watered by resilience and faith.

That's why seeing Liz meant so much. She reminded me of the little girl inside me who once wondered if such a life was possible, and of the woman who finally made it real.

If there is one truth I hope Liz carries with her, it is this: dreams are timeless. They do not expire with age, and the courage to pursue them never diminishes. Whether in childhood or adulthood, they remain alive as long as we nurture them. And when the right season arrives, their light guides us exactly where we are meant to be.

♥

WITHERED HANDS

U nderstanding disability requires more than noticing a difference. It means recognizing the challenges people face while also honoring their resilience, creativity, and dignity. Those who live with disability often invent new strategies for daily living, turning difficulty into quiet strength.

A withered hand can result from age, injury, illness, or a congenital condition. It may appear shrunken, twisted, or lack the strength and flexibility of a healthy hand. Yet behind what the eye sees lies a story of adaptation that speaks louder than appearance.

One day, while boarding, I noticed an older woman seated in the first-class cabin. She greeted me warmly and asked for coffee before takeoff. I served her cup and set it on the tray table. She reached for it without hesitation, holding it in a way that felt entirely natural to her. Later, as she unwrapped her food, I instinctively offered to open it for her. She declined with a kind smile.

Her movements carried a quiet grace. Watching her sip her coffee, I realized that what seemed unusual to me was, for her, simply life as she knew it. She was not defined by limitation, but by the creativity that allowed her to move through the world on her own terms. At that moment, I stopped seeing her hand as withered. I saw a woman who had mastered her own rhythm of living.

For people with a withered hand, resourcefulness often becomes second nature. Sometimes help is welcomed. Other times, independence is carefully guarded. What makes the difference is not only the hand itself, but also the way others respond — with assumptions, pity, or genuine respect.

It is easy to notice what is missing. Making the most out of life despite what's missing takes great skill and adaptation. Adaptation is a form of artistry. Acceptance is its foundation. And pride often grows quietly in the balance between limitation and possibility.

The world may never fully understand the journey of someone living with disability. But if we pause long enough, we can see that within their daily actions lies a truth: limitation and possibility are not opposites. They can coexist, shaping lives that are both ordinary and extraordinary.

♥

WHEN THE WORLD STOPPED FLYING

"World Surpasses 35 Million Cases of COVID-19."
"Major U.S. Airlines Continue Slashing Service During
Coronavirus Outbreak: We Will Get Through This."
"How Airlines Are Dealing with the Coronavirus Outbreak."

Headlines like these flooded our screens in early 2020, each one heavy with uncertainty and fear. They forced a question into the open: Was the world ready for this? Most of us felt unprepared, overwhelmed by shock, sadness, and confusion. Each morning began with grim updates, and the constant news cycle became an emotional weight. I often felt low, but I reminded myself to focus on resilience rather than despair. This was our new reality, whether we were ready for it or not.

The early months of 2020 brought a cloud of doubt. Jobs were at risk. Health felt fragile. Families feared for loved ones, and communities faced isolation. For those of us in aviation, the blow was especially sharp. Airlines struggled to survive as demand collapsed. Airports, once alive with movement, grew eerily quiet. Planes sat grounded. I took voluntary unpaid leave; many of my colleagues did too, while some others took early retirement. Others faced devastating layoffs. A few airlines could not recover at all.

Even small changes symbolized the magnitude of the shift. At first, wearing a mask at work felt foreign and uncomfortable. Eventually, it became second nature, a simple act of safety in a world that felt unsafe. Hospitals, meanwhile, reached breaking points. Medical staff bore the crushing weight of overflowing wards. Families grieved as lives were lost at an alarming rate. The stillness of empty terminals reflected not only halted travel but also the collective pause of humanity.

When my employer asked how the pandemic had affected me, I chose to be honest. I spoke about my love for flying and about finding light amid the dark. The crisis forced me to reframe my perspective, and in that space, creativity took root. Out of loss came the inspiration for my second book, *I Love Flying*, a tribute to the aviation industry and to those we lost during the pandemic. Writing became a way to honor resilience and hold on to hope.

The pandemic left each of us with lessons, though not the same ones. Some learned the fragility of health. Others rediscovered family bonds. Many of us, including myself, were reminded of how deeply connected we all are. Simple routines — shopping, traveling, gathering with friends — suddenly felt like luxuries. Loneliness magnified the value of community. Checking on neighbors, sharing resources, or offering kind words became vital acts of survival and solidarity.

Personally, I reevaluated my relationship with time and with myself. The forced stillness made me notice joys I had overlooked before: a calm morning, time to journal, the rhythm of quiet reflection. Technology bridged the gap with loved ones, but I also learned to lean into solitude, finding growth in it rather than resistance.

As restrictions eased and life slowly reopened, I carried those lessons with me. Gratitude became more than a word—it became a practice. Adaptability turned into strength. Empathy felt essential, not optional. Though the scars of loss remain, they sit beside a deeper awareness of endurance and the beauty of moving forward.

When the world stopped flying, we learned how fragile life can be. However, we also learned about the resilience of the human spirit. The sky did not stay silent forever. And when the engines roared again, they carried not only passengers but also new perspectives, shaped by a time that tested us all.

UNEXPECTED SOLITUDE

In 2020 and 2021, global travel slowed to a crawl. Airlines that had once been symbols of freedom and connection suddenly looked fragile. Entire fleets sat grounded. Schedules shifted without warning. Flights were canceled by the thousands. The industry that had promised adventure and discovery was now associated with risk, constant testing, and the uneasy question: what happens if today is the day the results come back positive?

For flight attendants, uncertainty became routine. The job that once gave me the world now asks me to live with caution. Would this flight expose me to a disease? Would I stay in a hotel for one night or a week? The pandemic had already stripped us of so much, and still we pressed on, day after day, under new rules and risks.

It was in this environment that I began what should have been a normal four-day trip. The schedule looked familiar. I left early from a crowded JFK terminal, checked in with the crew, and prepared for the usual boarding rush. Nothing in the morning suggested that this trip would be any different. Yet by the time we reached Raleigh, North Carolina, I felt an unfamiliar weight pressing into my chest. My body seemed more tired than usual, and no amount of coffee or willpower could shake the fatigue.

At first, I brushed it aside. Flight attendants learn to work through aches, exhaustion, and the occasional cold. Fatigue feels like part of the uniform. But over the hours, my symptoms deepened: a scratchy throat, a rising fever, and a voice inside me insisting that something wasn't right.

My friend, Nestor, who works for Delta, at the gate, handed me a COVID-19 test kit. I told myself it was only a precaution, a way to quiet the doubt. But when two red lines appeared, there was no ignoring them. I had tested positive. For the first time, I was grounded not by weather, not by maintenance, but by illness.

Management moved quickly. A hotel room was booked for me in Raleigh, and I was told to isolate for five days. The company covered my food for the first three days, and my daughter, Mary, kindly delivered supplies at the start. What I expected to be a routine layover turned into forced solitude, and for someone used to constant motion, the stillness felt unnatural.

The first day passed in denial. I answered texts, scrolled through the news, and pretended it was a normal evening in a hotel room. By the second day, fatigue had me pinned to the bed. I slept long stretches, woke sluggish, and returned to sleep again. The computer stayed closed. My body made it clear: rest was not optional.

In the quiet, small rhythms emerged. Meals left at my door became markers of time. The sunrise and sunset framed each day. The view from my window showed planes still taking off and landing, their paths uninterrupted, while mine was paused. The contrast was sharp: the world outside moving, my world inside still.

There were moments of fear. Would my symptoms worsen?

Would I become one of those stories on the news? Alone in that room, it was easy for the mind to spin through every possibility. There were moments of loneliness, too. Flight attendants live in a constant community — crews, passengers, hotel lobbies buzzing with familiar noise. The silence of the room felt heavy, broken only by the hum of the air conditioner or a plane's descent outside.

But in the stillness, clarity also found me. With nothing pulling me in a dozen directions, I opened a book I had carried for months but never finished. I began journaling again, something I had neglected in the rush of trips. I tried home remedies — garlic with honey, hot teas, small rituals of care that reminded me of simpler times. Meals became slower and more mindful, not quick bites between flights.

Isolation taught me the weight of inactivity, too. By the fourth day, my legs were swollen from lying in bed. I realized how harsh extended stillness can be on the body, just as much as constant movement. Balance was something I had rarely considered before.

The experience revealed both sides of solitude. On one hand, it was healing. My body recovered. My mind, stripped of distractions, had room to breathe. On the other hand, it was humbling. Humans are built for connection, and separation — especially when forced — carries risk. Too much solitude can slip into emptiness, anxiety, and emotional disconnection.

The pandemic magnified these truths for everyone, not just for those of us in aviation. Illness, grief, and personal trials can isolate anyone. We saw how solitude can either renew us or erode us, depending on how long it lasts and what we do within it.

For airline workers, this lesson carried extra weight. Our lives revolve around movement, community, and connection. To be stopped in place was more than inconvenient — it challenged our sense of identity. Yet in Raleigh, I learned that being still could also reveal strength. Isolation was not just an absence. It was space. And in that space, I began to see myself more clearly.

When the five days ended, I stepped back into the rhythm of airports and flights. But I carried with me something unexpected: the knowledge that solitude, though painful, can also be a teacher. It reminded me of my vulnerability and my resilience. It taught me to value small connections, to pay attention to my body's needs, and to accept rest without guilt.

The aviation industry has since recovered. Airports are loud again, flights are full, and the hum of global movement is back. But those quiet hotel days remain etched in me. They remind me that strength is not always about pushing forward. Sometimes it is about being willing to stop, to listen, and to heal.

Unexpected solitude showed me that even when the world pauses, the journey does not end. It shifts. And in the silence, we discover a different kind of flight — one inward, toward resilience, renewal, and the hope that tomorrow will open its doors again.

♥

GIVE ME A SMILE

During the height of the COVID-19 pandemic, our world became a place of hidden faces. Masks covered our smiles, muffled our voices, and created invisible barriers between strangers who were already keeping their distance. For someone whose job depends on connecting with passengers, this felt like trying to speak a language with half the words missing.

That's why the passenger in seat 15B stood out so dramatically on that flight to Atlanta, Georgia. While everyone else sat quietly behind their masks, he radiated an energy that seemed to light up the entire back section of the plane. Every time I walked down the aisle, he would catch my eye and gesture enthusiastically.

"Hey, give me a smile!" he would call out cheerfully. "I can see it in your eyes even with that mask on!" His own eyes crinkled with evident joy, and despite everything — the restrictions, the tensions of that time, the exhaustion we all felt — I found myself genuinely smiling beneath my mask.

"You know what I miss most about this whole pandemic?" he told me during one of my walks through the cabin. "Seeing people's full faces. Smiles are contagious, and we're all walking around like we're hiding from each other. But you — you've got kind eyes. I can tell you're smiling even when I can't see it."

His observation stayed with me throughout that flight and long after. Here was someone who refused to let a global pandemic diminish his commitment to human connection. He had learned to read smiles in eyes alone, to find joy in a time when joy felt scarce, and most importantly, to actively encourage others to keep smiling even when no one could see it.

That encounter changed how I approached every flight afterward. I realized that during those masked months, our eyes had to work double-time to convey warmth, humor, and reassurance. A smile might be hidden, but the energy behind it—the genuine care for another person's wellbeing—could still shine through.

Research confirms what that passenger intuitively knew: smiling activates neural pathways that boost mood, reduce stress, and create instant connections with others. Even when forced, smiles trick our brains into feeling happier. But more than the science, that passenger taught me something simpler and more profound—that choosing joy, especially in difficult times, is a gift we give not just to ourselves but to everyone around us.

Now, whenever I greet passengers, I remember his lesson. Some passengers smile back immediately, others engage in conversation, and some choose to keep to themselves. But I've learned that offering a smile—whether visible or hidden behind a mask—plants a seed of positivity that can bloom in unexpected ways.

The pandemic has changed many things, but that cheerful passenger reminded me that our fundamental need for human warmth remains constant. In a world that often feels disconnected, a simple smile becomes a small act of rebellion against isolation, a gentle insistence that we are all in this together.

Sometimes the most powerful gestures are the simplest ones. A smile costs nothing, requires no special skill, and can be given freely to anyone. Yet it has the power to transform moments, ease tensions, and remind us that beneath our various masks—literal or metaphorical—we are all hoping for the same thing: to feel seen, welcomed, and valued by our fellow travelers through life.

STRUCK BY LIGHTNING

Lightning strikes on airplanes are dramatic. It might seem frightening, but lightning hitting an aircraft isn't as catastrophic as many imagine. Thanks to engineering, training, and procedural rigor, these strikes are rarely dangerous. By understanding the science behind them and the safety measures in place, travelers can gain confidence that lightning, like many challenges of flight, has become a manageable part of modern aviation.

I experienced this firsthand during a flight from Raleigh-Durham to Boston, Massachusetts. While sitting in my jumpseat, a sudden flash of light filled the window in the cabin. For a moment, I froze. It was my first time seeing lightning hit our aircraft, and I felt a rush of nerves. The flash was so quick, yet so powerful, that it left my heart racing. Passengers nearby noticed too. Some turned toward me with wide eyes and anxious faces, silently asking if everything was alright.

I had to steady myself, shift my thoughts, and take a calming breath. I reminded myself of my training and compared the flash to a camera bulb—bright, startling, but gone in an instant. Quietly, I prayed for our safety and focused on reassuring the passengers with a calm expression.

The captain soon confirmed that our plane was in no danger and that we could safely continue to Boston. His steady voice reminded us of what we already knew: aircraft are designed to handle lightning. What could have been a stressful memory instead became a shared story, one that ended with our crew enjoying a warm dinner together, courtesy of our generous captain. Even a turbulent day feels lighter when you have a strong crew by your side.

Later, I decided to learn more so I could answer passengers' questions if this happened again. Here's what I found. Modern airplanes are designed with lightning in mind. The principle of the **Faraday cage** is central to this protection. A Faraday cage is a conductive enclosure that channels electrical charge across its surface, shielding whatever is inside. Airplanes work the same way. When lightning strikes, the charge usually enters through the nose or a wingtip, travels harmlessly along the fuselage, and exits through another point. Inside the cabin, passengers might notice a bright flash or hear a faint thud, but little else.

Despite advanced weather technology and route planning, airplanes are struck by lightning every day around the world. At cruising altitude, aircraft are constantly exposed to charged environments. Still, there have been no crashes directly caused by lightning on modern airliners in decades. Engineers, pilots, and regulators have refined designs and procedures so that what looks frightening to the eye is actually a controlled, well-prepared-for event.

That lesson stays with me. Just as airplanes are built to withstand actual lightning, we too must learn to endure life's sudden shocks. Strikes—both literal and metaphorical—will always come. Preparation, perspective, and trust in what we know help us move forward, even when the sky feels uncertain.

Life can flash with unexpected moments, just as lightning lights up the night sky. We may not be able to stop them, but we can choose how to respond. Calm, trained, and grounded, we can ride through the turbulence and land safely on the other side.

THE FLIGHT NOT TAKEN

Failure is the moment when plans collapse, expectations fall apart, and the outcomes we hoped for slip just out of reach. Yet failure is not final. It is a threshold, a pause that allows new possibilities to emerge. Its lessons are hard-won, but they teach resilience, humility, and the courage to rise again.

That day in Savannah, Georgia, I thought everything was going according to plan. Boarding was nearly finished, the cabin door was about to close, and I was already imagining an on-time departure. The weather was kind, the mood in the cabin light. Everything felt routine, almost too routine, as if nothing could possibly go wrong.

Then three young men walked onto the plane together. At first glance, they seemed like typical friends traveling side by side. But one of them immediately caught my attention. His steps were heavy, his shoulders slouched, his face pale. Something about the way he moved told me that all was not well. He lagged behind his companions, making his way down the aisle with a kind of weariness that seemed unusual for someone so young.

I made a mental note to check on him once everyone was seated. Sure enough, after boarding was complete, I walked toward his row. His head was pressed against the tray table, his body still and withdrawn. I gently asked if he was feeling alright. Before he could answer, his body reacted violently. He vomited suddenly — half on himself, half across the floor of the aircraft. The sound and smell spread instantly, triggering a ripple of alarm from the nearby passengers. Some turned away in disgust, others in sympathy, but all recognized that something had just changed.

It was no longer a routine afternoon. I knew in that moment that our flight would not be leaving on time.

I quickly moved to support him, my training and instinct taking over. His two friends explained quietly that they had all just come from military school. I could tell they were worried but also embarrassed, as though the incident reflected on them as well. The young man's condition was clear — he could not remain onboard. The decision was not his to make. It was one dictated by health, safety, and the well-being of everyone else on the plane.

I guided him gently up the aisle, steadying him as we walked. With each step, more of the unpleasant evidence followed us. Behind us, the cleaning crew began their own work of cleaning and preparing the space again, but I stayed focused on the young man. At the jetbridge, the gate agent was waiting. Her words were calm but final: "You won't be able to fly today. We need to make sure you're well enough to travel."

He didn't argue. He simply stood there, defeated. His silence was louder than any words could have been.

Then, almost in a whisper, the gate agent leaned toward me and shared something that pierced through the moment: he had not passed his training at the military school. He was being sent home, not as a cadet in progress, but as a young man whose future had suddenly shifted.

In that moment, my heart broke for him. He was about the same age as my son. I imagined the weight he was carrying — not just the sickness in his body, but the failure he felt pressing down on his spirit. Military school might have been his dream, his chosen path, his proof of worth. Now it was gone. The academy that once symbolized discipline, purpose, and pride was now a closed door, and he stood on the other side of it, uncertain of what lay ahead.

Once the cabin was sanitized, we closed the door and prepared for departure. I walked back down the aisle, the smell of disinfectant mixing with the stale reminder of what had just happened. Passengers shifted back into their seats, relief spreading as normalcy returned. By the time we leveled off above the clouds, the cabin had regained its calm rhythm. But my thoughts remained fixed on the young man left behind.

Failure often feels like that — being left standing at the gate while others take off. It isolates you, makes you feel exposed, and fills you with questions you cannot answer. Where do I go now? What do I do next? Who am I without the dream I just lost?

I thought about my own failures. The doors that closed unexpectedly. The flights in life I thought I was meant to take but never boarded. Each of those moments left a scar. Yet, in time, I realized they also opened new paths. They forced me to discover parts of myself I never would have known otherwise. They taught me to redefine success, not by what I achieved instantly, but by how I endured setbacks and kept moving forward.

That young man reminded me that failure is universal. We all stumble. We all face doors that refuse to open. But just because one flight is not taken does not mean the journey is canceled. Sometimes, being grounded is the first step toward discovering a better route.

I do not know where life will take him. But I hope, as he stands in the silence of disappointment, he will one day see another door waiting for him. And when he steps through it, he will realize that the flight he lost was not the end, but the beginning of something new.

The true measure of our journey is not found in perfect schedules or smooth departures. It is in the way we rise again when things go wrong. Like a delayed flight, like a journey interrupted, failure only pauses us. It does not define us.

And I hope, for him and for all of us, that the flights we don't take will one day lead us toward the ones we were meant to board.

♥

BOUNDARY AT 35,000 FEET

T he early afternoon sun cast its rays across the tarmac as passengers filed toward the jetbridge, their steps filled with the anticipation of travel. Among them was a mother, standing stiff and alert, with her young daughter by her side. The girl, no more than six years old, clutched a small bag in both hands, her face glowing with excitement.

I greeted them warmly as they approached, offering a smile and a gentle, welcoming tone. "Welcome aboard!" I leaned forward slightly, hoping to capture the little girl's attention and reassure her. My hand lifted instinctively, intending to rest lightly on her shoulder for a moment of comfort.

Before I could reach her, the mother's voice cut through the air. Sharp. Firm. Final. "Don't touch her, we do not know you!"

Her eyes narrowed, her posture tense, as if her words were not only for me but for everyone within earshot. My hand froze mid-air. My face betrayed a flicker of shock before I masked it with a professional calm. Still, my brown skin flushed red, heat rising to my cheeks. My colleague beside me noticed immediately and quietly suggested I sit down for a moment to breathe.

The sting of her words lingered. My emotions ran their course in familiar sequence: surprise, discomfort, reflection, and finally, resilience. At first, I felt hurt—my small act of kindness had been received as something almost dangerous. But soon, I reminded myself that in this job, I must adapt quickly. Every passenger brings their own boundaries, their own histories, their own fears.

I asked myself what had fueled her reaction. Had my gesture crossed an invisible cultural line? Did her own past experiences lead her to see danger in what I thought was reassurance? Or was it simply a worldview that saw strangers—even flight attendants—as potential threats? Whatever the reason, she had drawn her boundary with unmistakable clarity.

As the flight continued, I noticed her body gradually relax. The steady hum of the aircraft, the smooth service in the cabin, and the professionalism I maintained began to ease her nerves. Later, she asked me for a drink. This time, her request came with a quiet "thank you," her voice softer, less brittle. It was a small shift, but enough to signal that her wall was lowering, even if only slightly.

Her response stayed with me. A mother has every right to protect her child. Boundaries matter, especially in a world where safety can never be taken for granted. Yet I also realized something important: boundaries can be set without hostility. Protection does not require rudeness. Trust can be safeguarded without cutting others down. A calm word, a clear explanation, or even a firm but gentle reminder can draw the same line while leaving dignity intact on both sides.

As flight attendants, we are asked to do more than serve drinks or ensure safety protocols. We carry the responsibility of emotional agility, adjusting to the unpredictable moods, fears, and expectations of hundreds of strangers at 35,000 feet. Some interactions are easy; others are difficult. But each one leaves a mark, shaping the journey as much as the destinations we fly to.

That day, I learned again that kindness may not always be welcomed, and gestures of comfort may sometimes meet resistance. Yet the lesson was not about withholding warmth, but about offering it with greater awareness. Boundaries must be respected. Kindness must sometimes take quieter forms.

When I am asked about rude passengers, this memory is the one that surfaces. Not because it was the worst moment, but because it carried meaning. It reminded me that travel is not only about moving through the skies, but also about moving through the fragile, unseen spaces of human interaction. At 35,000 feet, we are not just passengers and crew—we are strangers sharing a journey. And how we treat each other along the way makes all the difference.

♥

OH NO, I SPILLED THE COFFEE!

In the complex, choreographed world of air travel, flight attendants do far more than pass out snacks and beverages. Our work demands precision, situational awareness, and an ability to stay calm under pressure — because even the smallest slip can ripple through the cabin. Carefulness isn't just a nice trait; it's the foundation for passenger comfort, safety, and trust.

It was a calm flight, the kind that lulls passengers into their movies and naps. Seat 10B was occupied by a gentleman I'll call Mr. Ron — smartly dressed in a navy polo and pressed slacks, fully absorbed in a film on his phone. The cabin had that rare, peaceful hum, and I was gliding down the aisle with my service cart, focused and efficient, but secretly enjoying the rhythm of the moment.

When I reached Mr. Ron, I gave my usual warm smile and asked, "Coffee, tea, soda, or juice?" "Coffee, please," he replied with a polite nod.

I poured the steaming brew into the cup, placed it carefully on his tray table… and then disaster struck. In a moment that felt both painfully slow and far too fast, my hand brushed the cup's rim, tipping it just enough to send a wave of hot coffee cascading onto Mr. Ron's perfectly pressed slacks.

My heart plummeted. My face turned as red as the aircraft exit signs. "Oh my goodness, sir — I am *so* sorry!" I exclaimed, grabbing napkins as quickly as possible. The nearby passengers looked over with curiosity, some with sympathy, others with the quiet drama only an in-flight mishap can inspire.

But here's where the story turned. Mr. Ron looked down at his soaked slacks, then looked up at me with a calm smile. No anger, no irritation — just grace. He accepted the napkins, patted at his pants, and quietly walked to the restroom to clean up. When he returned, I offered another heartfelt apology and said, "Thank you for your understanding, sir. I'm honestly so embarrassed for the trouble I caused." I added service recovery points to his account, hoping to express how much I appreciated his patience.

That flight became unforgettable — not because of my embarrassment, but because of Mr. Ron's reaction. His quiet kindness turned a potentially awkward moment into something unexpectedly heartwarming.

This was the first and only time in my ten years of flying that I spilled coffee on a passenger — and I'll never forget it. Not just because it was a rare mistake, but because it reminded me that compassion goes both ways. In a job where we are constantly trained to serve and to soothe, it's humbling and beautiful when a passenger ends up being the one who shows grace.

As I think back on that day, I can't help but smile. Mr. Ron probably remembers the flight attendant who spilled coffee on him, but I'll always remember the gentleman who wore his coffee-stained slacks like a badge of patience. He taught me that a little grace can turn even a hot mess — literally — into a small, shared story of humanity.

QUALITY TIME

Q uality time, even in small doses, has a way of weaving threads of connection that last far beyond the moment. It's not about spending endless hours together; it's about being truly present — listening, laughing, and letting each other know that we matter. In a world where work, schedules, and responsibilities pull us in a hundred directions, those moments of presence become precious treasures.

One bright Tuesday after landing in New York, I found myself with a few hours of free time before my next flight. Instead of retreating to a quiet corner with my coffee or catching up on sleep, my heart longed for my children. I picked up my phone and typed a hopeful message: *"Lunch today, if you're not busy?"*

Within minutes, Mary replied with an enthusiastic yes, and Joshua sent a simple thumbs-up that made me smile. The thought of seeing my kids — even just for a quick meal — was enough to turn an ordinary layover into the highlight of my week.

We agreed to meet at a Filipino restaurant halfway between their neighborhood and JFK. It was one of our favorites, a cozy spot that always reminded us of home. When I saw Mary and Joshua walk through the door, my heart swelled. Their hugs were familiar yet always fresh — a reminder that no matter how far I travel, I belong with them.

We ordered our favorite dishes and laughed as we shared stories, catching up on the little details of each other's lives. For me, these meals are more than food; they are nourishment for my soul, filling the spaces that distance leaves behind.

Of course, no family gathering is complete without our tradition of taking pictures — something my children never let me skip. Those snapshots become my companions when I'm flying through the friendly skies, each image tucked safely in my heart.

Time slipped away faster than I realized. When I glanced at my watch, panic fluttered in my chest — my flight was less than two hours away, and I still needed to take the subway back to the airport.

"I hate to say it, but I have to rush!" I said, reluctantly gathering my things.

We stepped outside, and I hugged Mary and Joshua tightly, wishing I could hold them just a little longer. My heart was full, but my feet had to move. I sprinted to the subway, racing through the station and boarding the train, my mind counting down the stops like a silent prayer.

I made it back to the airport just in time for boarding — breathless, anxious, but grateful. Grateful for the chance to pause in the middle of a busy day, to be mom first and flight attendant second, if only for a little while.

Over the years, my job has taken me across oceans and mountains, introduced me to thousands of passengers, and given me countless stories. But no view from 35,000 feet compares to sitting across the table from my children, hearing about their lives, sharing laughter, and being reminded of what truly matters.

Through all the arrivals and departures, I've learned that love is not measured in hours, but in the quality of time we share. Those lunches, those brief reunions — they are proof that even in a busy life, we can still make room for love, presence, and connection.

THE ART OF GIVING

Even the smallest acts of kindness — a word, a gesture, a helping hand — can ripple outward in ways we never expect. Sometimes, the most ordinary moments hold the greatest opportunities to make a difference.

One quiet morning in Syracuse, New York, I sat down with a simple plate of eggs and toast in the hotel dining room. The air smelled of freshly brewed coffee, and the clatter of dishes mixed with the low hum of conversation. A staff member named Melissa walked by, and her eyes caught on the scarf around my neck.

"That's beautiful," she said softly, her voice warm but tinged with exhaustion.

I smiled, touched by the compliment. The scarf was soft, pink, and vibrant — a recent gift from a dear friend in the Philippines. It had quickly become one of my favorite travel companions, wrapping me in comfort on long layovers and reminding me of home.

Melissa lingered for a moment, then began to share pieces of her story. "My brother is sick," she said, her voice faltering. "He's in the hospital, and he's in a lot of pain." As she spoke, her worry poured out — sleepless nights, unanswered questions, the heavy helplessness of watching a loved one suffer.

I listened, setting aside my fork and giving her my full attention. In that moment, the world outside seemed to fall away. We were just two women, strangers only minutes ago, connected by the invisible thread of empathy.

When Melissa returned to her work, I sat in silence for a few minutes, reflecting. The scarf around my neck wasn't just fabric — it was a gift, a token of care from a friend who had thought of me. But now, as Melissa's words echoed in my mind, I sensed it could become something more.

I thought of the frame hanging on my bedroom wall, engraved with the words: *Life is not about doing great things, but doing small things in a great way.* That scarf could be one of those "small things."

Rising from my seat, I carefully folded the scarf and made my way to the kitchen. Melissa looked surprised to see me.

"For you," I said, holding it out. "I hope it brings you a little comfort."

Her eyes widened. "Are you sure? It's so beautiful."

"Yes," I said with a smile. "It was given to me as a gift, and now I'd like to pass this gift along to you."

She took the scarf slowly, almost reverently, her face softening as tears welled in her eyes. That small exchange — that moment of giving — filled the room with quiet gratitude.

Later, our pilot told me that Melissa had been telling everyone at the hotel about the scarf. It wasn't just a piece of fabric to her — it was a reminder that kindness still exists in the middle of hard days.

For me, that scarf became more meaningful after I gave it away than it ever was when I owned it. It reminded me that giving isn't about offering something extravagant or perfect. It's about sharing what we already have, even if it costs us a little — and sometimes, especially if it does.

As I travel from city to city and country to country, I carry that lesson with me. I look for those small openings where a word, a smile, or a simple gift can lift someone's heart. Because the art of giving isn't measured by the size of the gift, but by the love and intention with which it's given.

MIRROR, MIRROR ON THE WALL

Psychologists often say that a mirror is one of the most powerful tools we have for seeing ourselves clearly. It invites self-awareness, encourages acceptance, and offers a kind of satisfaction that doesn't rely on anyone else's approval.

One of the hotels we frequently stay at has a unique mirror with the words *"Mirror, mirror on the wall"* etched along the frame. It always makes me smile because it calls to mind the Queen in *Snow White*, asking her mirror who was "the fairest of them all." Unlike the Queen, I'm not looking for someone to crown me the fairest. I'm seeking something deeper — a moment to center myself before stepping into the day.

My mornings follow a ritual as familiar as breathing. Coffee first — always coffee. Then a shower to wake me up, makeup to freshen my face, hair styled just right, shoes polished until they shine. I zip my luggage, making sure it carries not just my uniforms and essentials but also a piece of my spirit — the calm confidence I'll need once I step onto the plane.

Before leaving my hotel room, I do a mental sweep to make sure nothing is left behind. Then I pause in front of the mirror. This is where the ritual shifts from routine to intentional. I take a breath, square my shoulders, and begin my quiet self-talk:

"Today is a good day. I will greet passengers with kindness. I will embody grace. I will bring calm to the clouds."

I practice what I call the *Mirror Technique* — standing tall, head held high, looking not for flaws but for strength. It isn't vanity. It's a reminder that the woman staring back at me has weathered both literal turbulence in the sky and the storms of life below.

In college, my friends used to tease me for glancing at every reflective surface — shop windows and parked cars — as if I was obsessed with my reflection. Back then, it was about appearance, about catching imperfections and adjusting what I could. Sometimes it was self-consciousness, sometimes a little vanity.

But somewhere along the way, my perspective shifted. Now, at 55, with more than a decade of flying behind me, I look in the mirror and see something different. I see a face that carries laugh lines, signs of wisdom, and traces of every mile traveled. I see resilience and compassion. I see a woman who has faced exhaustion, difficult passengers, and life's disappointments — and still shows up smiling.

The mirror no longer reflects just my appearance. It reflects my journey — every challenge that shaped me, every kindness that kept me going. True beauty, I've learned, isn't measured by age or smoothness of skin but by character.

Every day, no matter where I am, I take those moments with the mirror seriously. I speak gratitude over my day, courage into my heart, and strength into my posture. When I finally walk out the door, I am not just ready to serve passengers — I am ready to meet the world as my most authentic self.

MY CELEBRITY BOO-BOO

Life has a clever sense of humor. Just when we think we have our plans lined up perfectly, it delights in flipping the script and surprising us in ways we never imagined. What started as a weekend of disappointment over missing a long-awaited concert for *my favorite idol* became one of the most humbling and unexpectedly meaningful encounters of my life—a moment that reminded me that even our idols are simply human.

For weeks, I had been looking forward to seeing one of my favorite singers perform live in Nashville, Tennessee. Her voice had been the soundtrack of my childhood, her songs woven into birthday parties, road trips, and countless quiet nights spent dreaming about the future. I planned to finally see her on stage, in all her glory, under the glittering lights. But life, as it often does, had other plans. A last-minute schedule change meant I would be in the air, working a flight, instead of in the crowd, singing along with thousands of other fans.

I'll admit, I was a little down as I prepared the galley that weekend. But then something extraordinary happened—one of those quiet miracles that life sprinkles in just when you need it most.

As I was arranging the coffee pots and snack baskets, the gate agent arrived with our very first passenger. She was elegant, almost regal, draped in a luxurious fur coat and carrying a stylish purse. There was no entourage, no flashing cameras, just a woman who moved with quiet confidence. She gently hung up her own coat in the closet and settled into seat 1A without asking for any special treatment.

I greeted her with my usual warmth and offered her a drink. "Is Nashville home for you?" I asked casually, expecting the usual polite reply.

"No, I'm here for a concert," she said, her voice soft and melodic.

Something about her voice made me pause, but I didn't think much of it until the gate agent, with a little sparkle in her eye, leaned toward me and whispered, "That's Diana Ross."

My heart skipped a beat. *Diana Ross.* The very person I had been so disappointed about missing was sitting right in front of me—calm, elegant, and close enough that I could hear her breathing. I felt like I had stepped into a dream.

I couldn't keep this to myself, so I quietly told my flight attendant partner and asked if she could help me get a photo. After mustering my courage, I approached Diana with the most polite, respectful request I could manage.

She listened to me, smiled faintly, and shook her head. "I don't take pictures," she said simply.

Her words were kind, but they landed like a tiny pinprick to my heart. I could feel my cheeks warming with embarrassment. I had been so excited, so sure this would be my chance to capture the memory forever. Instead, I found myself retreating, fighting back a mix of disappointment and awkwardness.

But life has a way of softening even the most tender moments. Later in the flight, Diana asked to borrow a pen. I gladly handed her mine, and when she was done, she tried to give it back. I shook my head. "Keep it," I said. It was just a pen, but to me, it felt like a small offering—my way of saying thank you for sharing this moment with me, even without the photo.

Diana remained quiet throughout the flight, dignified and serene. She didn't ask for snacks or drinks, never called for attention. When we landed in Nashville, she deplaned as gracefully as she had boarded. After she left, I noticed a few candy wrappers tucked by her seat—an oddly human touch that made me smile. Even the most glamorous legends have their quiet little habits.

On my way home, I thought about the entire encounter. At first, I felt the sting of missing a once-in-a-lifetime photo opportunity. But as I replayed the memory, I began to see it differently. The stage lights, the applause, the perfection we imagine when we think of our idols—those are just parts of the picture. Behind them is a person, just like us, who values her privacy, who eats candy, who sits quietly when she travels, who sometimes just wants to be a passenger and not a superstar.

That day taught me that true admiration is not about collecting proof—pictures, signatures, or stories to share on social media. True admiration respects the human behind the legend. Diana Ross didn't owe me a photo, but she gave me something far more meaningful: a memory that lives in my heart, unfiltered and completely real.

Even now, whenever I hear my favorite song of hers, *Do You Know Where You're Going To*, I smile. Not because I got the perfect selfie, but because I didn't. That moment became more than just a fan encounter — it became a gentle reminder that even the brightest stars need space to just be.

I may have missed the concert lights, but I walked away with a story I will cherish forever. My little "celebrity boo-boo" turned out to be a blessing — a lesson in humility, respect, and remembering that no matter how iconic someone may seem, they are still wonderfully, beautifully human.

♥

WHEN TURBULENCE
HAPPENS

High above the clouds, the world feels like a gentle cradle—until it doesn't. On one particular flight headed for New York, my day began much like any other. The passengers were comfortably seated, the cabin lights glowed softly, and the service moved along without a hitch. The aroma of freshly brewed coffee mingled with the quiet chatter of passengers, and I moved gracefully down the aisle, pouring coffee, offering drinks and snacks, and sharing the kind of small, reassuring smiles that make a flight feel safe and familiar.

Just as the cart was nearly empty and the cabin had settled into a peaceful hum, the plane gave a sudden, sharp jolt. It wasn't the mild sway we experience so often, but a strong tremor that made me pause mid-step. Before I could fully react, the captain's calm voice filled the cabin:

"Ladies and gentlemen, we are experiencing unexpected turbulence. Please fasten your seatbelts."

I have heard those words countless times, yet each time my pulse quickens just a bit. The familiar bumps and rattles remind us that the sky is not always still—but this was more than gentle rocking. The aircraft shuddered with a persistence that made it clear: this was no quick shake.

My hands gripped the service cart tightly. I glanced around the cabin and caught the wide-eyed stares of a few passengers, their hands gripping armrests, silently seeking reassurance. Others squeezed their eyes shut, waiting for it to pass.

Training took over. I hurried toward the galley, quickly stowed the cart, and double-checked that everything was locked and secure. Even as my steps quickened, my mind ran through the checklist drilled into me during safety training: *remain calm, secure the cabin, check for compliance.*

Finally, I strapped myself into the jumpseat. The turbulence rattled through the cabin. I inhaled deeply, reminding myself— and, in spirit, the passengers—that turbulence was normal, and the pilots were trained to navigate it safely.

When the shaking finally eased, a quiet collective sigh rippled through the cabin. The other flight attendant and I exchanged a quick nod and unbuckled. We moved through the rows, checking on each passenger. "Is everyone alright?" I asked gently, scanning faces for signs of distress.

In row 17, a mother sat with her two remarkably calm children. Gratitude shone in the mother's eyes as she said, "We're okay. The children are smiling. It's almost as if nothing happened."

Her youngest, a little girl clutching a well-loved plush toy, waved it at me with a wide grin, as if the turbulence had been just another part of her adventure. The toy, soft and slightly worn, had clearly been hugged through every bump. In that moment, it struck me how such small objects can anchor a child's heart, providing a sense of safety when the world feels out of control.

Nearby, a few passengers chuckled as they told their seatmates about drinks that had taken flight mid-air, pointing to droplets still clinging to the ceiling. That laughter—gentle and almost relieved—was the sound of tension melting away.

Turbulence affects people in very different ways. For adults, it often triggers memories of past flights, hidden fears, or sudden thoughts of what could go wrong. For children, it can be frightening—but they are also surprisingly resilient. Surrounded by the comfort of a parent's touch and the familiar feel of a toy in their hands, they recover faster than we do. Their ability to smile so soon after the shaking stops is a quiet kind of bravery.

As I returned to the galley, I thought about how turbulence is so much like life. We plan our routes, prepare our schedules, and hope for smooth sailing. But inevitably, the air grows rough. Illness comes, plans change, disappointments crash into our carefully laid timelines. We are jolted out of comfort and forced to hold on until the shaking stops.

And yet, just as in flight, we are equipped for these moments. Preparation—whether through training, wisdom, or faith—helps us stay grounded. Connection matters too: the presence of others reminds us that we are not alone. Sometimes, even a small object—a cherished photograph or a favorite plush toy—becomes the anchor that helps us ride out the storm.

When we landed safely in New York, I glanced once more at row 17. The children were giggling, their plush toy tucked under one arm as if it, too, had made it through a great adventure. They didn't deny what had happened—they celebrated that they had endured it.

That day reminded me that turbulence isn't just a travel hazard—it's a teacher. It shows us our strength, encourages us to prepare, and pushes us to be present for one another.

So, what can we do when turbulence—literal or metaphorical—strikes?

- **Know the Procedures:** Just as flight attendants are trained for turbulence, we can prepare strategies for life's surprises. Knowing what steps to take reduces panic.

- **Prioritize Safety and Well-being:** On a plane, this means fastening seatbelts. In life, it means seeking help, practicing self-care, and staying grounded.

- **Stay Calm and Present:** Fear thrives on uncertainty. Deep breaths and steady thoughts keep us from spiraling.

- **Find Comfort in Connection:** Family, friends, or even a small token of comfort can remind us that we are not alone.

- **Embrace the Unpredictable:** Some things can't be avoided. Accepting that we cannot control everything helps us respond with grace.

- **Foster Optimism and Resilience:** Like children with their plush toy, we can choose hope and keep smiling until the skies clear.

Now, whenever I face turbulence—whether in the sky or in life—I think of that little girl in row 17, clutching her toy and smiling wide, and I am reminded that no matter how rough the journey is, we can land with courage and joy.

A MENTOR'S TALE

B eing a mentor means guiding someone through their successes and failures — walking alongside them not just when the path is smooth, but when it twists, turns, and threatens to collapse under their feet. Every mentor is inevitably shaped by those they guide; their struggles become lessons, their victories a shared joy, and their hopes a mirror that reflects back our own aspirations.

I have always had a passion for guiding others, which is why I embraced the special assignment of being a mentor — a role I cherished for nearly two years. Mentoring was never just a duty to me but a calling, something I pursued with care and devotion, whether during quiet days off or late at night after a long shift. It was work that went beyond answering questions or giving advice; it was about being present, seeing potential, and walking through life's challenges together.

Among my mentees was Bailey, a bright and promising young woman eager to carve out a successful career in the skies. She was hardworking, full of life, and determined to prove herself. But life's lessons can sometimes arrive in the most heartbreaking ways. One morning, I saw her sitting quietly in the crew room, shoulders slumped, her face pale. I sensed something was wrong and gently asked if she was okay. She looked at me with tears in her eyes and asked to speak privately.

"I had a random alcohol test," she whispered, her voice barely audible, "and I failed the test."

For me, those words landed like a punch. My heart sank, and for a moment, I just stood there, frozen. I felt like her mother in that instant — protective, heartbroken, and wishing I could shield her from the consequences that were about to follow. This wasn't just a setback; it meant her career, which had only just begun, was effectively over.

At that moment, my role as a mentor became painfully clear. Mentorship wasn't about giving pep talks when things were going well — it was about standing with someone in the middle of their storm. I listened as she spoke, her voice trembling with fear and regret, and I could feel the weight of her shame pressing heavily on her.

Instead of scolding or lecturing her, I gave her what she needed most: understanding. We sat together in silence, letting the moment settle. I couldn't rescue her from the consequences, and it wasn't my place to try. But I could help her face them with dignity.

I reminded her gently that mistakes, while costly, are not the end of the story. They are often our greatest teachers. They strip us of illusions, show us where our judgment faltered, and point us toward growth — if we are willing to learn.

The aftermath of Bailey's mistake wasn't meant to define her forever. It was a painful pause, yes, but also a chance to begin again. Beginning again isn't about pretending the past didn't happen or brushing aside the hurt. It's about acknowledging it, learning from it, and giving yourself permission to rise again, stronger and wiser than before. That, I told her, was the essence of resilience.

Bailey's story reminded me how fragile dreams can be, how easily they can be shaken by a single moment of poor judgment. But it also reminded me that life is generous with second chances — if we are brave enough to take them.

That day, I learned something about mentorship: it isn't just about helping people climb higher. Sometimes, it's about holding space for their tears, standing with them in silence, and reminding them that they are not alone, even when the answers are out of reach. Mentorship is as much about presence as it is about guidance.

♥

WAKE ME UP, PLEASE!

L ife at 35,000 feet demands much from those who live it. The hours are long, the schedules unpredictable, and the physical toll undeniable. Yet for those who love it, the sky is never the limit — it is a calling, an endless horizon.

One night, that calling took the form of a storm system sweeping across the Midwest. The weather disrupted flights, shifted schedules, and drained the energy of everyone waiting inside Minneapolis–Saint Paul International Airport. My flight to Rochester, Minnesota, appeared on the departure board with its usual confidence. Then came the first delay, followed by another, and another. Minutes turned to hours. Each tick of my watch felt heavier as midnight crept closer.

The once-bustling terminal thinned out. Shops closed their gates, cleaners worked silently in the background, and the sound of rolling suitcases faded. By the time clearance came, more than three hours had passed. Well past midnight, the aircraft pushed back from the gate, and engines roared to life. The short flight to Rochester was smooth, the cabin quiet, most passengers sleeping, grateful to be in the air.

When we landed, the city lights blinked below us, small and steady in the early hours. The wheels touched down gently — a kindness after such a long night. By the time I checked into the hotel, it was 2:00 AM. The streets outside were silent, the world asleep. I went through my nightly routine on autopilot and fell into bed by 3:00 AM, my body sinking gratefully into the dark silence of the room.

This wasn't unusual. In aviation, delays are inevitable. Weather, maintenance, or crew changes can turn even the smoothest day into a puzzle of moving parts. Flexibility isn't optional; it is survival. Over time, I've learned that frustration only drains energy, while adaptability keeps me moving forward. The unpredictability isn't a burden anymore—it has become part of the adventure, part of the story I chose when I became a flight attendant.

I set my alarm for nine, just six hours away, knowing I needed to be back at the airport by ten. Sleep is precious on trips like these, rationed like water in a desert. But as dawn broke over Rochester, my body stirred earlier than expected. Years of training and habit have taught me not to fully trust alarms. Somewhere deep inside, a kind of built-in paranoia keeps flight attendants alert. We know that missing a wake-up call isn't just a mistake—it could disrupt an entire day of flights. My body, even when exhausted, refused to take the risk.

There was one thing I longed for before anything else: coffee. Not just any coffee, but the kind strong enough to cut through the fog of sleepless nights and endless delays. I made my way to the coffee table in the hotel lobby, following the familiar aroma. For me, coffee is more than a morning ritual. It is a reset button, a liquid reassurance that no matter how tired I am, I can find my footing again. The warmth in my hands, the bitterness on my tongue, the steam rising gently — it all works together to remind me that a new day is beginning.

Sipping that first cup, I felt the fatigue of the night still tugging at me, but I also felt something else: renewal. Coffee doesn't erase exhaustion, but it awakens resilience. It tells the body and mind, "Wake up. There's work to do. There's life to live." That cup became my quiet transition from night's chaos into morning's routine.

At the airport, the day unfolded as so many do: passengers juggling their own frustrations, announcements echoing over loudspeakers, and gate changes causing ripples of confusion. Flight attendants learn quickly that adaptability is more than a skill — it is an art. Some days require patience, others humor, and often both. We learn to sleep on command, to store energy in short bursts, and to keep going when most people would rather stop.

Just like every other job, being a flight attendant has its ups and downs. Delays test tempers. Exhaustion creeps in. Passengers sometimes misplace their kindness in the rush of travel. Yet within all of this, there are small victories that keep us steady. A smooth landing. A heartfelt thank-you. A brief conversation that reminds us of the connections we make every day.

These moments matter because they remind us why we keep showing up. For me, the reason is simple: I love flying. I love the friendships that form among crew members, the stories passengers share in fleeting moments, and the sense of being part of something larger than myself. Each day in the skies offers a new challenge, but also a new memory, a new story to tell.

If I didn't love this work, the weight of its demands would be unbearable. Love is what transforms exhaustion into commitment, delays into patience, and early mornings into opportunities. Alongside love, I carry two essentials: coffee and flexibility. They sound simple, but in this profession, they are priceless.

As I walked through the terminal that morning, steady steps carrying me forward, I felt the familiar mix of fatigue and gratitude. Another long night had passed. Another day had begun. And with it, another chance to embrace the unpredictability that defines this life. Each delay, each challenge, and each new dawn remind me that aviation isn't just about getting from one place to another. It's about resilience, connection, and the promise that even after the longest nights, there is always a morning waiting to wake us up.

♥

ON BEING NICE

I n this job, being nice is more than a smile or a polite greeting. It is empathy. It is patience. It is the ability to anticipate passengers' needs while maintaining safety and efficiency in a tightly structured environment. Being nice is also wisdom — the ability to know when kindness must be balanced with firmness, when compassion must coexist with clear boundaries.

A few months after training, I stepped into my first winter flying season. The memory is still vivid: a cold December morning, icy winds rushing through the jetbridge as passengers filed into the cabin. My assignment was a four-day trip alongside a senior, seasoned flight attendant. I was eager to learn, eager to prove myself, and most of all eager to embody the warmth and care I had been trained to show.

Passengers entered bundled in thick coats, dragging bags that seemed heavier with each step. Some looked weary from early-morning travel, others grateful just to board and find their seats. I greeted them with energy and warmth, offering to take coats and stow them in the cramped first-class compartment. The space was limited, but I carefully arranged each coat and bag, doing my best to make everyone feel welcomed and comfortable.

After a few minutes, the other flight attendant approached me. His voice was low, but his tone was firm: "Stop being nice.

Don't try to accommodate all the luggage and coats in such a small compartment—there's only so much space, and they're just too lazy to stow their stuff."

The words hit me like cold water. I froze, unsure how to respond, my instinct to defend myself tangled with my respect for his seniority. In the end, I nodded and continued working. Yet the exchange stayed with me long after that flight. It forced me to reflect: What does it really mean to be nice in this profession?

For me, kindness cannot be reduced to empty gestures. It is not about saying "yes" to every request or bending rules until they break. True kindness respects both the person and the system. It is about acknowledging each passenger as a human being worthy of respect—whether they are seated in first class or the last row, whether they arrive cheerful or irritable, whether they are seasoned travelers or nervous first-timers.

Kindness is often small and subtle. It is offering a blanket to someone shivering before they even ask. It is handing a passenger a bottle of water during a long delay. It is noticing the silent anxiety of a traveler gripping the armrest and offering reassurance. It is crouching down to help a parent struggling with children and luggage, or leaning closer to speak gently with someone who is elderly or unwell. These gestures cost little but mean a great deal. They turn a routine transaction into a human connection.

Over time, though, I learned the other side of kindness: boundaries. Passengers sometimes ask for things that are not possible—requests that conflict with safety procedures, company policies, or the realities of limited space and resources. Early in my career, I struggled with saying no. It felt unkind. But I learned that true kindness does not always mean giving in. Sometimes, it means explaining with empathy why something cannot be done, or offering an alternative that meets the need in a different way.

This balance — between generosity and firmness, warmth and professionalism — is the art of being a flight attendant. Without boundaries, kindness collapses into chaos. Without kindness, rules feel cold and impersonal. The strength of our role lies in blending the two.

I have also come to see that personality and character are not fixed. They are shaped by culture, education, experience, and the environments we navigate. Each crew member brings different strengths to the team. Some bring humor, some calm, some efficiency, and some meticulous organization. What matters most is not uniformity but unity — the ability to work as a team with professionalism and respect, even when personalities differ.

Being nice is a form of discipline. It requires self-awareness, emotional intelligence, and resilience. It asks us to keep our composure in the face of rudeness, to show patience when exhaustion presses in, and to hold empathy even when it is not reciprocated. It is not a weakness but a strength — the kind of strength that allows us to make hundreds of strangers feel safe and cared for in a metal tube 35,000 feet in the air.

Looking back at that cold December flight, I no longer see the senior flight attendant's warning as purely negative. In his blunt way, he was teaching me a lesson I needed to learn. Space is limited. Time is limited. Energy is limited. To serve well, I had to conserve those resources wisely. His words reminded me that kindness must be grounded in practicality. It cannot ignore reality; it must work within it.

Today, when I think about being nice, I no longer imagine it as endless accommodation. I imagine it as a balance: a balance between care and clarity, between warmth and authority, between generosity and boundaries. That balance leaves a lasting impression on passengers and colleagues alike.

Every day in the air is an opportunity to practice this discipline. A smile, a kind word, a patient explanation—all of these ripple outward, shaping the atmosphere of the cabin. At cruising altitude, kindness transforms the routine into something more: a shared experience of dignity, care, and connection.

For passengers, the flight may be one chapter in a larger journey. For us, it is another day at work. But the way we choose to carry ourselves—how we balance niceness with professionalism—can turn that chapter into a memory worth keeping. And in the end, that is what makes being nice at 35,000 feet not just important, but essential.

♥

A CHALLENGE COIN

Receiving a special gift from a stranger at an unexpected moment is a rare and shining kind of recognition – one that quietly integrates into the rhythm of everyday life and leaves a lasting impression on the soul. These moments serve as gentle affirmations that our actions, presence, or spirit have been noticed, valued, and cherished.

During a flight from JFK to Charleston, South Carolina, a serious-looking man in first-class asked me for tea, and we struck up a conversation about my airplane pendant. He called it a "900 plane" he'd flown with the U.S. Air Force, and our conversation flowed effortlessly from there. We talked about his military service, visits to the Clark and Subic bases in the Philippines, his international sports travels, and my previous job at the U.S. Department of Veterans Affairs in Manila. The nostalgia was palpable, reminding me of many fond memories of my homeland.

As our conversation drew to a close, he surprised me by pulling out a United States Air Force coin with his name, USAF Brigadier General Harvey W. Schiller, engraved on it. "Do you know the history of giving this to someone?" he asked, his eyes sparkling with curiosity. I admitted I didn't, and he smiled as he handed it to me. "It's a tradition," he said implicitly, his gesture speaking volumes. I thanked him sincerely, feeling a deep sense of gratitude.

As we chatted further, I mentioned my upcoming retirement, and he asked about my plans. "I'll travel the world and write more books," I replied. His eyes lit up, and he said, "I want to write a book, but I need to push myself to do it." I joked that I'd hold him to that, and we both laughed.

After the flight, I researched his distinguished career and was impressed by his numerous awards and accolades. As a retired Air Force Brigadier General, president of Turner Sports, and chairman and CEO of YankeeNets, he'd earned several military honors, including Air Medals, the Legion of Merit, and a Distinguished Flying Cross.

I also learned about the tradition of challenge coins, which originated in the military as a way to instill unit pride, improve esprit de corps, and reward hard work and excellence. These pocket-sized medallions are given as tokens of affiliation, support, patronage, respect, honor, and gratitude.

Receiving the challenge coin from Mr. Schiller was an honor, and I appreciated the genuine gesture behind it. It reminded me that curiosity, kindness, and dedication can build bonds that transcend titles and professions. The unexpected nature of his gift made it even more meaningful – it wasn't given out of obligation, but out of genuine gratitude and support.

We stayed in touch, and I shared with him that my story about meeting him would be part of my flight attendant book. He said,

"Congratulations, ten years of service and a youngster at that. Hope our paths cross again. Waiting to read your book."

SEEING BEYOND FIRST IMPRESSIONS

J udging others is almost instinctive. Our minds are quick to size people up, often in a matter of seconds. We notice their clothes, their tone of voice, their expressions, and without realizing it, we place them into categories. These snap judgments may feel natural, but they often cloud our perceptions and limit our ability to connect authentically. Every person we encounter carries a unique story, unseen struggles, and layers of experience that go far beyond a single moment.

I once read these words: *"Not judging is a gift we can give to others."* The truth of that statement lingers with me. Choosing to withhold judgment is like opening a door—it invites empathy, compassion, and connection where there might otherwise be distance.

I was reminded of this during a simple encounter on a flight. While serving snacks, a middle-aged woman smiled warmly and complimented my hair. "I like your hair and bun," she said. Her kindness made me smile. As part of the service, I offered her cookies. She took one, tasted it, and said, "I love these cookies." So, I gave her an extra one, happy to see her delight in something so small.

Later, after we landed, she waited until most passengers had deplaned before approaching me again. She introduced herself as a traveling nurse and said, "You're so nice." I thanked her and, almost in passing, mentioned that I would be retiring in June. She looked at me and asked, "Oh, is that why you're nice?"

The comment caught me off guard. It was one of those remarks that sits at the edge of compliment and judgment, uncertain in its intention. In that moment, I had a choice: to take offense, to defend myself, or simply to let it pass. I chose to smile, holding onto the kindness of our earlier exchange rather than the sharpness of her last words. After all, everyone is entitled to their perspective, and I had no idea what kind of day she had before stepping onto that flight.

That interaction made me reflect on how easy it is to misinterpret someone else's words or actions. Sometimes what feels like judgment may come from a place of curiosity, fatigue, or even insecurity. Other times, it may reveal more about the speaker than the one being spoken to.

Judging others isn't just a personal flaw — it can have ripple effects. It shapes how we treat one another, how communities form, and even how cultures divide. Psychology Today describes two main ways we interpret people's behavior: **situational attribution** and **personality attribution.** Situational attribution considers the circumstances — what might be happening around the person that influences their actions. Personality attribution, on the other hand, assumes behavior stems directly from character.

Most of us, without thinking, lean toward personality attribution. We assume someone is rude, careless, or lazy, rather than wondering if they're tired, worried, or facing unseen challenges. Research shows that people tend to overvalue personality traits and underestimate situational factors, especially when encountering strangers. Our brains are wired for speed, not nuance, so we take shortcuts. But the more aware we become of this tendency, the more intentional we can be about offering grace.

I don't exempt myself from this struggle. There are times I rush to judge, only to realize later that I misunderstood the situation. Reflecting on those moments has taught me to slow down and give others the benefit of the doubt. Instead of assuming the worst, I try to ask myself: *What might this person be going through? What story don't I see?*

Holding back judgment isn't about silencing our thoughts or pretending differences don't exist. It's about humility—choosing to recognize that we rarely see the whole picture. It's about compassion—allowing others the space to be human without labeling them too quickly.

When we withhold judgment, something powerful happens. A pause creates room for empathy. That pause might turn an ordinary exchange into a meaningful connection. It allows us to see not just the surface, but the heart. And in that space of empathy, respect, and kindness take root.

The lesson is simple but not easy: before we judge, pause. Before we assume, consider. Before we label, listen.

Because when we look at people not through the lens of judgment but through the lens of understanding, we begin to see the humanity that connects us all. And in that shift, each encounter—no matter how brief—becomes more meaningful, leaving behind a memory of kindness rather than a scar of criticism.

WHAT IF NO ONE IS WATCHING?

There are moments in life when the simplest choices challenge the very core of who we are. Sometimes, the test does not arrive with loud alarms or flashing lights. It arrives quietly, tucked into the ordinary, when no one is looking.

For me, one such test came during a flight from Cincinnati, Ohio, to Austin, Texas. I had worked dozens of flights that month, each with its own rhythm, yet this one would stay with me far longer than the rest.

As the passengers boarded and the cabin settled, I moved gracefully down the aisle, my presence attentive but calm. With years of experience, I had learned to sense moods before words were spoken, to anticipate needs before requests were made. My eyes caught details: a restless foot tapping, hands fidgeting with a boarding pass, a glance that lingered too long on the safety information card. Each gesture told a story.

When the beverage service began, a gentleman seated by the window caught my attention. His hands trembled slightly as he placed his order. "Whiskey," he said quietly, almost as though asking for something forbidden. The nerves in his eyes gave him away. I had seen that look before — the tight jaw, the forced composure of someone uneasy with flying.

I retrieved the small bottle, offered a cup with ice, and opened the seal for him. As I placed the drink on his tray, his fingers brushed mine, and he quickly pressed a crisp five-dollar bill into my hand. "Thank you," he whispered, gratitude clear in his voice.

For a moment, I froze. Tips were not allowed. We had been taught this from the very beginning: serving passengers was part of our role, not a service to be rewarded like in a restaurant. I smiled and shook my head softly. "I appreciate it, but we're not supposed to take tips," I said.

The passenger hesitated, his eyes darting briefly around the cabin. Then he leaned slightly forward, lowered his voice, and asked, "What if no one is watching?"

That question landed heavily. My fingers tightened around the cup in my hand. What if no one was watching? It was a five-dollar bill. Nothing extraordinary, but still a test. For me, taking it wasn't an option. Not because I'm flawless, but because I know where I draw the line. In that moment, I thought back on the choices I've made over the years. Times when I stayed honest even if no one was watching. Times when I followed what mattered, even while quietly setting aside smaller rules that didn't always make sense. I am not perfect. But I knew this wasn't mine to take. Integrity, I had learned, is not just a habit. It is a foundation. It is who you are when no one is watching.

I returned the bill gently to his tray table and met his eyes with a smile. "I'm retiring next month after ten years of flying," I told him. "At this point in my career, I don't want to jeopardize my service over a five-dollar bill, even if no one is watching."

Something in my response must have reached him. His shoulders softened, his tight posture eased, and his eyes grew less guarded. He picked up his cup, took a slow sip, and then confided in me with a voice almost lost in the hum of the engines. "I'm on my way to Austin to see my mother," he said. "She's getting old. This might be the last time I see her."

That confession shifted the moment. The tip was no longer the story. His trembling hands were not just about flying; they were about fear, about grief, about the weight of saying goodbye.

I leaned slightly closer, offering quiet advice to ease his flight. I spoke of small things—steady breathing, focusing on the rhythm of the engines, remembering that turbulence is uncomfortable but rarely dangerous. My words seemed to ground him, but our conversation soon drifted to something deeper: the things that matter most in life.

We spoke of family, of honesty, of the courage it takes to do the right thing when no one is watching. And in his words about his aging mother, I heard something universal—a reminder of how fleeting time with our loved ones truly is.

The truth is that many of us postpone visits, waiting for the "right time" that never seems to come. We assume our parents will always be there, holding the same place in our lives they always have. But aging does not wait. As our parents grow older, their health shifts, and suddenly, the visits we had delayed become impossible.

For an aging parent, our presence is more than a courtesy. It is an affirmation that their life, their years, their sacrifices still matter. Sitting with them, listening to the same stories for the hundredth time, holding their hand even when words fail — these are not small things. They are acts of love that reach deeper than any gift we could buy. They create memories that outlive us, memories we cling to when the final goodbye arrives.

That flight from Cincinnati to Austin ended as all flights do — with passengers gathering their belongings, the cabin filling with the rustle of coats and bags, and goodbyes exchanged at the door. But for me, the moment with the nervous flyer lingered.

I thought about his question long after we landed: "What if no one is watching?" It was about a tip that lasted only seconds, but it was also about life itself. Every day, we face choices that seem minor, choices no one else may ever know about. Do we cut corners when unseen? Do we act kindly only when others will notice? Do we keep promises only when someone holds us accountable?

Integrity is not built in the public eye. It is built in the quiet moments, in the decisions we make when no one applauds, when no spotlight shines, when no one is watching. Those choices shape us. They prepare us for the bigger tests that life will inevitably bring.

And as for love, it too is built in quiet moments — the unplanned visits, the held hands, the hours spent listening. Just as integrity shows who we are when unseen, love shows its strength in the presence we give when it would be easier to stay away.

The man's story about his aging mother reminded me that flights, like life, are temporary. Each has a beginning, a middle, and an end. We do not control how long the journey lasts, but we do control how we show up during it.

So when I think back on that day, I realize the real lesson was not about money, or rules, or even anxiety about flying. It was about the character we choose to live with. Integrity and love are built the same way: one small choice at a time, often in silence, often when no one is watching.

And for those blessed with aging parents, the greatest choice is presence. Each visit tells them, without words, that they are still cherished. Each hug, each conversation, each shared meal becomes a reminder that they are not forgotten. When the final goodbye comes—and it always does—it is those choices, those visits, that remain.

That flight ended like any other, but the question still echoes in my mind. What if no one is watching? The answer is simple: who you are in those moments is who you truly are.

IMPERFECTION VERSUS PASSION

Flying isn't just my job; it is my heartbeat. It is how I measure the passing of time, how I feel the rhythm of my days and nights, and how I anchor myself in a world that is constantly moving. The sky has been my workplace, my sanctuary, and my second home.

Yet there is one place where my grace and confidence stumble: the kitchen. Cooking has never been my gift. For me, it feels more like a chore to be avoided than an art to be mastered. My family and friends know this well, and they tease me with affection about my "culinary crimes." I laugh with them, shrugging off my reputation as the "worst cook" with humor and humility. After all, I love food—especially Mexican cuisine—but I love being a diner much more than being a chef.

One Friday evening, craving tacos, I decided to defy my reputation. Hunger and rare confidence collided, and I thought, why not try? I had made tacos before. What could go wrong?

The answer was: plenty.

In my small Jacksonville apartment, I set a frying pan on the stove and poured a generous splash of olive oil. The kitchen felt warm, almost too warm, but I didn't pay much attention. A phone ping distracted me. By the time I returned to the stove, the oil shimmered, nearly boiling. Without thinking, I dumped the marinated beef into the pan.

The eruption was instant. The hot oil hissed violently, spitting and splashing onto my left hand and leg. I yelped, dropping the spatula as the sting spread in sharp waves across my skin. Panic took over. The smell of scorched oil filled the room, mixing with the sharp sting of pain.

I froze for a moment, fear rising. Alone in my apartment, I felt the sudden weight of vulnerability. The kitchen around me seemed to shrink as the pain grew sharper. My hand throbbed, my skin angry and red. The situation could have spiraled into fear, but instinct kicked in. Trembling, I grabbed my phone and searched: "First aid for oil burns."

The instructions were simple: run cool water over the burn. I rushed to the shower, letting the water flow over my hand and leg. The cool stream dulled the heat, but tears came anyway — tears of pain, but also of frustration and embarrassment. Thirty minutes passed before I could peel myself away. My skin was blistered, my pride scorched.

Wrapped in a towel, I stood in front of the bathroom mirror, staring at my hand. It looked raw and angry, a visible mark of my failure in the kitchen. My daughter, concerned, urged me to go to urgent care and even offered to pay for it. But in my stubbornness, I told myself I could handle it. I drove to the nearest drugstore instead, picking up ointments, gauze, bandages, and pain medication.

The next morning, the swelling had worsened. I was flying to New York, but I squeezed in a doctor's visit before my trip. The diagnosis was quick: a second-degree burn. The doctor dressed the wound, offered kind reassurance, and told me to rest.

But rest is not part of my vocabulary. I am right-handed, and though the bandages slowed me, I could still manage. Showering, dressing, and buttoning my uniform took longer, and simple routines became obstacles. Yet I refused to take sick leave. Flying was not just a job—it was my joy, my purpose, my lifeline. I was not willing to stay grounded because of one accident.

Onboard, passengers noticed the heavy bandage on my hand. Some offered sympathy, others asked questions. Instead of dwelling on the injury, I turned it into a joke. "Oh, I punched someone," I'd say with a grin. Or, "My cooking is so bad, even the stove fought back." Their laughter lightened the mood and eased my own self-consciousness.

But behind the humor was a quieter question: would the scar remain? Would this mark be a permanent reminder of my clumsiness? In the early days, I saw it that way—with embarrassment. But as time passed and my hand slowly healed, my perspective changed.

The burn became more than a sign of failure. It became a mark of resilience. A reminder that I was willing to try, willing to stumble, and still willing to move forward. My hand, though scarred, told a story—not of weakness, but of persistence.

Flying has always reminded me that passion outweighs perfection. The sky does not care if I can cook. My passengers do not measure my worth by my kitchen skills. What they see is the dedication I bring, the care I show, and the humor I use to turn pain into connection. My burn became part of that story —a quiet symbol of my priorities and resilience.

This experience taught me something simple but lasting: we all have flaws. For me, cooking is one of them. I can laugh about it, but I also know it will never be my strength. My passion, however, is flying. And passion gives me the strength to endure pain, to overcome setbacks, and to keep showing up with love for my work.

Scars, whether physical or invisible, do not diminish us. They shape us. They remind us of battles faced, lessons learned, and the courage to try again. My burn taught me that perfection is an illusion, but passion is real.

This story is not about culinary disaster or physical pain. It is about the victory of the spirit. It is about finding humor in mistakes, determination in hardship, and love in the work we choose.

So now, when life puts me in hot water—whether in the kitchen or in the skies—I remind myself: mistakes happen, wounds heal, scars remain, but passion endures.

Our imperfections do not hold us back. They point us toward the things that matter most. And when we choose passion over perfection, we find joy not just in what we do, but in who we become.

♥

BETWEEN SKIES AND STORIES

Since 2014, I have worn my wings with pride, declaring, "This is it. This is my retirement job." I loved the rhythm of airports, the hum of engines, and the ever-changing skies. But while I soared from city to city, another passion was quietly brewing beneath my uniform. It was a passion that consumed my time, thoughts, and emotions: the craft of writing.

Long before travelers and colleagues knew me as "Lia, the flight attendant," I was already a storyteller. I wrote blogs about my life adventures. I created reports that highlighted people's good deeds. I wrote quirky pieces as a CNN iReporter. I even reported news as a freelance writer for Allvoices. Through World Pulse, I connected with people across borders, sharing stories and knowledge that touched lives far beyond my own. Before I ever took to the skies, my words had already traveled further than I could have imagined, carried to readers in places I had never set foot.

Still, I harbored a secret dream—one I had lovingly sketched onto my vision board. Among the photos of places to visit and things to acquire, I tucked in a drawing of a book. I gave it a title I had imagined years earlier. That small drawing was more than a doodle. It was a declaration to myself. I deeply believed in the power of manifestation, in the quiet magic of visualizing what could be, until the universe conspired to make it real. Each glance at that vision board felt like a promise: one day, I will be an author.

What I needed wasn't just an idea but the right spark of inspiration. In 2019, as autumn shifted into winter, the moment arrived quietly yet with the weight of destiny. An idea, long dormant, began to stir inside me. During flights and layovers, I carried my laptop like an extra piece of luggage. Early mornings when sleep escaped me, I would sit by hotel windows, tapping away as city lights faded into dawn. At night, when the world outside was silent, my mind would race with stories until I had no choice but to write them down.

I still remember one layover in New York. The city was alive with holiday lights, but instead of going out with my colleagues, I stayed in my room. I ordered a sandwich, opened my laptop, and typed for hours until my eyes grew heavy. Another time, in Syracuse, while snow blanketed the streets, I spent the night editing and rewriting until it felt right. These small choices — the ones no one else noticed — were the bricks that built my dream.

For five months, I lived inside my manuscript. I wrote, edited, and rewrote, sometimes at airports, sometimes in coffee shops, often in the stillness of hotel rooms. Determination fueled me. The sharp focus that had always guided my work as a flight attendant now became my strength as a writer. I sacrificed sleep, leisure, and social events, but I never doubted the journey was worth it.

Then came March 2020. I held my book in my hands for the first time. The cover gleamed under the light, and my name was printed boldly across it. The rush of pride and gratitude was indescribable. I had become the author of *What We Know For Sure: Inspirational Stories of Filipino Special Immigrants in America.* My success wasn't luck. It was the result of pairing clear intention with relentless effort.

That moment taught me something that has stayed with me: goals matter. My vision board had been more than decoration. It had been a compass. Without that drawing of a book, without that visible reminder of my dream, I might never have found the courage or focus to follow through.

A goal is not just a destination. It is a compass that points us forward when uncertainty surrounds us. It reminds us why we keep going even when we are tired. Setting a goal gives us something to aim for beyond the routine of daily life. Writing my book was not only about the final product. It was about the person I became along the way—a more disciplined, creative, and resilient version of myself.

Here are ways you can achieve your goals:

- **Visualize Your Success:** Create a vision board or write down your goals. Seeing them daily keeps them alive in your mind. My book began as a small drawing I looked at every day until it became a reality.

- **Break Down Big Dreams:** Large ambitions can feel overwhelming. Break your goal into smaller, manageable steps. I didn't think of writing an entire book at once. I thought of writing one page, then one story, until the manuscript was done.

- **Be Adaptable:** Circumstances will shift. In airports, hotel rooms, and on planes, I learned to write anywhere and anytime. Progress matters more than perfect conditions.

- **Make Time:** Waiting for the "right" moment means waiting forever. Use the time you already have. Write during breaks, study on your commute, practice during quiet hours. Those small pockets of effort accumulate.

- **Find or Cultivate Inspiration:** Surround yourself with people, places, and habits that fuel your drive. For me, inspiration came from the stories of my former colleagues at the American Embassy, whose courage to immigrate I wanted to honor.

- **Stay Determined:** Perseverance is the bridge between dreams and reality. Work toward your goal every day, even if progress feels slow. Consistency wins over intensity.

Manifestation is often misunderstood as wishful thinking. But for me, it was about belief paired with action. I didn't just imagine the book. I visualized it so clearly that it felt inevitable, then backed that vision with daily effort. Manifestation created a feedback loop: faith fueled my actions, and my actions reinforced my faith. By practicing manifestation, I trained my mind to recognize opportunities and to stay positive, even when exhaustion or doubt crept in.

As flight attendants, our schedules include breaks that can feel like pauses in the middle of a busy life. Yet those pauses can open doors. They can become spaces for discovery, growth, or creation. Whether your dream is to write, study, learn a skill, start a business, or launch a new career, your free moments can be stepping stones.

For me, hotel rooms became writing retreats. Quiet flights became brainstorming sessions. Airport lounges became editing offices. What others might see as downtime, I used as preparation for my future.

Your dream may be waiting for you to do the same.

If you have a vision in your heart, start today. Don't wait for the perfect moment or permission. Visualize your goal, write it down, and work on it every day. The path will not always be easy, but persistence makes progress possible.

The sky isn't the limit; it is only a perspective. What matters is not how high you fly but how true you remain to the dreams you carry. All it takes is a vision, the courage to begin, and the perseverance to see it through.

Between skies and stories, I discovered that both can carry you far. One takes you across the world. The other takes you deeper into yourself. And both remind you that with faith and determination, the dream you once drew on paper can one day rest in your hands.

♥

PRAYER IN MY POCKET

In the world of aviation, a flight attendant's journey is defined not only by the destinations we reach but also by the challenges we overcome along the way. Each flight is more than a routine—it is a testament to preparation, resilience, and dedication.

Many are drawn to this profession by its elegance: serving passengers with poise, visiting cities and countries that only exist on maps for most people, and forming bonds with fellow crew members that feel like family. Yet, behind the smiles and sparkling service lies a rigorous responsibility. Each flight attendant must recertify their qualifications annually, a process called Continuing Qualification. This test isn't just a formality—it evaluates our mastery of emergency procedures, safety protocols, and customer service. Failing is not an option; if we don't pass, we cannot fly until we do. The stakes are high, and the pressure can feel overwhelming.

For me, Continuing Qualification is both a technical challenge and a personal test of endurance. I prepare meticulously. As soon as the online modules are released, I dive into the material, refusing to leave anything to chance. I know procrastination is an enemy, so I plan early, reviewing, practicing, and internalizing each step. Yet, no matter how much preparation I do, the night before the assessment, a familiar knot of nerves tightens in my chest, swirling like turbulence on a stormy flight.

But I have a secret: a prayer in my pocket. It is a small token of faith, something I've carried with me since the very beginning of my career. It isn't just an object—it's a reminder of hope, courage, and trust that preparation, combined with faith, will see me through. When doubt creeps in, the prayer is my anchor.

I think back to Minneapolis, Minnesota, in 2014, during my initial training. I was 44, surrounded by classmates much younger than me, and the days were long and grueling. Written exams loomed every other day, hands-on drills demanded precision, and the training manual seemed to grow heavier with each passing moment. It felt like running a marathon with no finish line in sight—my legs ached, my mind was fatigued, and my spirit sometimes wavered. Yet, I kept moving forward.

Every morning, I rose before the sun, determined to absorb as much knowledge as possible. I studied quietly, often sneaking into the bathroom to avoid waking my roommate, my prayer tucked safely in my pocket, whispering encouragement to myself. Occasionally, doubt would knock on my door: "Can you really do this? Are you too old for this intensity?" But each time, I silenced it, reminding myself that perseverance is forged through struggle.

Beyond the rigorous drills, the camaraderie of my classmates, encouragement from instructors, and shared stories of hardship and triumph became my lifeline. The training wasn't just about procedures—it was about discovering my own resilience, the strength that surfaces when the path is hardest.

The final exam day arrived with a surge of nervous energy. My heart pounded as I entered the testing room, clutching my prayer in my pocket. I breathed, steadied myself, and faced the challenge. When the results were announced, I had passed — not with perfect scores, but successfully. Overwhelming relief and joy washed over me. Tears streamed down my face, carrying a month of hard work, anxiety, and determination. During the graduation ceremony, I felt a profound gratitude for the journey, for the faith that had guided me, and for the inner strength I had discovered.

The prayer in my pocket is more than a charm — it is a symbol of trust in oneself and in a higher purpose. It reminds me that faith, combined with preparation, can guide us through uncertainty, lift us during moments of doubt, and empower us to persevere despite obstacles. For ten years, it has been my companion, silently encouraging me as I navigate the skies, ensuring I am grounded even at 35,000 feet.

Every journey — whether across continents or through personal struggles — begins with faith, courage, and the decision to move forward, one deliberate step at a time. And sometimes, that courage is quietly tucked into your pocket, waiting to remind you that you are capable of more than you know.

♥

DO YOU LOVE YOUR JOB?

L oving your job is more than just waking up each morning because you have to—it's about finding joy, fulfillment, and purpose in what you do. It means embracing your responsibilities with enthusiasm, facing challenges with a positive mindset, and feeling satisfaction not only in the results but in the process itself.

At its core, loving your job is about forming an emotional connection with your work. It's the quiet pride that swells when you finish a task well, the willingness to go the extra mile for a colleague or passenger, and the eagerness to turn ordinary moments into experiences of care and attention. It's about resilience, too; tough shifts, fatigue, and unexpected setbacks don't diminish your commitment. Instead, they become opportunities to grow, adapt, and find new ways to excel.

Passengers often ask me, "Do you love your job?" Without hesitation, I always reply, "Yes!" Their smiles and nods tell me that they sense my passion—it shows in my voice, my gestures, and my attention to detail.

Endeavor Air has recognized my dedication through an awards program, giving me "Excellence in Service" pins for achieving milestones. After only four months on the job, I received my first pin. The surprise filled me with pride and motivation, reminding me that what I do matters. Over the years, I earned four more pins, each representing a new letter of appreciation from passengers. These tokens aren't just awards — they're symbols of connection, gratitude, and purpose.

Fellow flight attendants ask how I maintain this level of recognition. My simple answer is, "I love what I do." It's a truth that carries me through long, unpredictable shifts, sudden schedule changes, and days when exhaustion threatens to take over. Love for the job transforms challenges into opportunities, and fatigue into determination.

Passengers have written heartfelt letters expressing their gratitude. One particularly memorable letter read:

"I would like to give a compliment to your flight attendant, Lia. She's absolutely wonderful, very pleasant, and cheerful during the whole flight. I noticed her working fast and well-organized to serve the passengers. It is admirable that she has such a great, positive attitude in handling and serving the passengers. I would definitely hire her if she's seeking a career at my company. Well done, Delta. You have a great employee. Thanks."

Moments like this are far more meaningful than awards alone. They affirm that the connection I create with passengers — through kindness, attentiveness, and empathy — is what makes this work fulfilling. The relationships, not just the accolades, fuel my passion.

I've also witnessed extraordinary dedication in my colleagues. One of them, my friend Evelyn, once went beyond her job description when she gently wiped an elderly passenger's hands after he used the bathroom. It was a small act, but a deeply human one, and not something she was required to do. And there was the captain who reached into a toilet bowl to retrieve a stranded roll of toilet paper. It was far from the duty expected of a captain, yet she did it without hesitation, showing a kind of humility and care that left an impression on all of us. These acts of care show that loving your job goes beyond duty; it becomes a mindset that permeates every action, no matter how small.

Loving your job means that effort never feels forced, even after long hours or sleepless nights. It means responding to unpredictability with understanding rather than frustration, and celebrating the joy of making someone's day a little brighter. It's a choice, a mindset, and a practice that radiates outward.

The benefits are profound. Passionate workers perform better, inspire colleagues, and create positive experiences for customers. Happiness increases, stress diminishes, and work becomes not just a job, but a source of purpose and fulfillment. Each letter, compliment, and award serves as a reminder: when work transcends duty and becomes passion, excellence, and joy follow naturally.

Loving your job doesn't just change your day — it transforms the way you impact others, the quality of service you provide, and the meaning you find in your life.

♥

"SHE CAN'T RETIRE!"

T hose words echoed in my mind, making me pause and reflect on how deeply we touch each other's lives, often without even realizing it.

It was the last flight of the day and the final leg of my four-day trip. Every crew member looks forward to "go-home day," silently praying for smooth skies, no delays, and no last-minute surprises.

Cincinnati has always been one of my favorite airports. It's small enough to navigate easily, calm even during busy hours, and filled with genuinely kind people. At the gate for our flight to JFK, I noticed an older woman in a wheelchair, her cane resting by her side. She was stunning in that effortless, graceful way age can bring. Her posture was poised, her expression serene, and her smile radiant.

When our eyes met, she offered me a warm smile, and I returned it instinctively.

She boarded first. As I helped her to her assigned seat, a middle row halfway down the cabin, I noticed several empty seats closer to the front. I quietly moved her there for a more comfortable ride. She thanked me with such gratitude that it lingered in the air between us.

Our conversation flowed easily, like two travelers sharing a small, unexpected moment of connection. There was something in her presence, a gentle strength, a light that spoke of storms survived.

"Are you heading home or visiting New York?" I asked, my usual icebreaker.

With a spark in her eyes, she said, "Oh, I love Delta! This is my first flight in five years. I had cancer, but I'm better now. I'm going to New York to see a friend perform in a musical!"

Her joy was contagious. Despite everything she had been through, she radiated life. I couldn't help but smile. "That's wonderful," I said. "Enjoy every moment of the show."

After ten years in this job, moments like these are what I cherish most: helping people, easing their travels, offering comfort where I can. Each encounter reminds me that kindness is never wasted. Every flight, every face, every small conversation has shaped me in ways I'll never forget.

When we landed at LaGuardia, I helped retrieve her bag and guided her back to her wheelchair. She smiled up at me and said, "I'm heading home Tuesday. Maybe I'll see you again."

I smiled and whispered, "I'm retiring next month."

She looked shocked. "You can't retire," she said, her voice full of warmth. "You're too nice."

Later, as I made my way through the terminal, my four-day trip finally over and ready to see my kids in New York, I ran into a pilot friend and stopped for a quick chat. Just as we finished talking, I caught sight of my passenger again. From across the crowd, she waved and called out, pointing toward me:

"She can't retire!"

We both laughed, and I waved back.

Her words stayed with me long after she disappeared into the crowd. I thought of all the passengers I've met over the years, people traveling for business, for pleasure, for healing, or for new beginnings. Each carried a story, and together they've filled my career with meaning.

Letting go of something you love is never easy. But as I counted down the days to my retirement, passengers like her reminded me why I loved this job in the first place. The memories, the kindness, the connections — they're treasures I'll carry with me forever.

And though I may be retiring, a part of me will always remain in the skies, where strangers meet, and kindness finds its quiet wings.

♥

EPILOGUE

WING RESTED, HEART SOARING

As I close this important chapter of my life, I look back on ten remarkable years in aviation—a decade filled with personal growth, professional milestones, and unforgettable human connections. The familiar hum of engines may now be just a memory, but the lessons I learned above the clouds remain deeply rooted in who I am. My career was never just about flying; it was about evolving as a person, embracing resilience, and discovering the beauty of connection in every encounter.

When asked why I chose to retire—especially at a relatively young age—I answer with confidence: change is not an ending, but a beginning. My decision was guided by intuition and deeply personal reasons. It may not be fully understood by everyone, but it is part of my journey, and I embrace it wholeheartedly.

Retirement does not diminish my love for aviation; if anything, it deepens my gratitude for every mile flown, every sunrise above the clouds, and every smile exchanged at 35,000 feet. As I step into new pursuits—whether through part-time work, new hobbies, writing more books, or traveling to new destinations—I carry forward the same spirit of curiosity, courage, and openness that defined my flying years.

I am profoundly grateful for all my experiences: the camaraderie of colleagues, the kindness of passengers, the laughter on long layovers, and the quiet moments of reassurance offered during turbulence. Each interaction left its imprint, teaching me that empathy and kindness are as essential in life as they are in the skies.

Documenting these memories has been both a reflection of gratitude and a way of leaving a legacy in the aviation world. Every flight symbolized beginnings and endings, joy and uncertainty—a reminder that life itself is a series of departures and arrivals, each shaping who we become.

Facing turbulence in the air prepared me for turbulence in life. I've learned that resilience is choosing courage over fear, and that even the smallest act of kindness can ripple far beyond its moment. These lessons, forged at altitude, will continue to guide me wherever life takes me next.

To everyone who shared this journey—colleagues, passengers, friends, and loved ones—I offer my deepest thanks. Your support, stories, and simple acts of connection reaffirmed the truth that we are all linked, even in fleeting encounters.

Letting go is not losing—it is making room for growth. Just as every journey eventually comes to an end, it also opens the runway for a new one. Change, like flying, requires trust in new possibilities and faith in horizons yet unseen.

As I take my final bow in this profession, I do so with a heart full of gratitude and eyes lifted toward what lies ahead. My hope is that the stories within this book inspire you to approach the world with curiosity, kindness, and wonder. Though my wings may rest, my heart continues to soar.

With love and gratitude, I wish you safe travels wherever your dreams may lead—and the courage to embrace each new horizon.

My last day at work in Syracuse, New York, on June 30, 2024

CONCLUSION

A s I look back on my years in the sky, I see more than just flights, layovers, and destinations. I see moments of connection, lessons learned in the aisles of airplanes, and life-changing encounters that stretched my heart and mind. The passengers, colleagues, and even strangers I met along the way became teachers in their own right, showing me the power of empathy, patience, and kindness.

Being a flight attendant is more than a career—it is a lens through which I've come to understand life itself. I've witnessed joy, sorrow, fear, and triumph at 35,000 feet, and in each experience, I discovered something about love, resilience, and the human spirit. From the simple comfort of a shared smile to the profound impact of a mentor's guidance, life in the sky has taught me that our choices and gestures ripple far beyond what we can see.

The skies are unpredictable, much like life. Turbulence, delays, and unexpected challenges are inevitable, but it is how we respond—with grace, courage, and love—that shapes our journey. My hope is that the stories I've shared will inspire you to navigate your own path intentionally, to treasure connections, and to embrace every opportunity for growth.

Life is fleeting, yet beautiful. Love fiercely, give generously, and approach each day as a chance to leave a mark—no matter how small—on the lives of others. Whether in the air or on the ground, the lessons I've learned remind me that we are all connected, and that our presence, however brief, can make a lasting difference.

Thank you for joining me on this journey through the skies. May your own journey be filled with purpose, courage, and the quiet joy of noticing the world—and people—around you.

ACKNOWLEDGEMENTS

With Gratitude — I Give You My Wings

As I close the chapter on my flight attendant career and bring this book's journey to a landing, I am reminded that every flight begins not only with two pilots but with the dedication of an entire crew, the quiet hum of anticipation in the cabin, and the steady, unseen guidance from those on the ground.

My deepest gratitude goes to **Endeavor Air and Delta Air Lines** — the runways where my dreams truly took flight. I am thankful for the opportunities and endless possibilities that connected my worlds. To the Endeavor Air flight attendants and pilots, whose professionalism and camaraderie were the tailwinds behind every joyful takeoff and safe landing — thank you. To my flight attendant friends, who filled long layovers with warmth, laughter, home-cooked recipes, and midnight confessions, the stories and moments we shared at 35,000 feet and beyond are treasures I will carry forever.

To every passenger who trusted me with their care, who laughed with me, smiled at me, and shared a story or a fleeting moment of wonder — thank you. You reminded me that love, like flight, knows no boundaries.

To my beloved children — **Jonathan and Agnes; Mary Frances and Franz; Joshua and Clarissa** — you are the wind beneath my wings. Your love and steady support have brightened even my darkest skies. To my grandchildren, **Shanel and Drake** — your curiosity and boundless energy give me strength and hope.

To **Amie Amaechi, my editor** — your creativity and thoughtful guidance have been the compass steering this book through clear skies. Your sharp editorial eye, paired with gentle encouragement, lifted these pages to new heights. I am deeply grateful for the care you invested in every word.

To **Jennalyn Natanauan, the artist behind the book**, thank you for bringing my vision to life with such beauty. Your artistry captures the spirit of this book, creating a cover that soars as high as the stories within.

To my family and friends — thank you for comforting me when the winds were fierce and for soaring with me when the skies were calm. Your unwavering support has carried me further than I ever imagined.

To my classmates, **Class 14-02** — thank you for sharing your dreams, whispering your fears in quiet corners of our training rooms, and standing together through long, challenging days. Our camaraderie gave each of us the courage to fly higher. To my training professors — thank you for instilling resilience, encouraging every step forward, and believing in us even when self-doubt whispered otherwise.

I am also grateful to the **recruitment and mentor teams**, who recognized something authentic in me and gave me the chance to share my skills and passion. To the **management team at JFK, New York**, my professional home for ten years, and to the **Association of Flight Attendants** —thank you for your dedication and support.

To the colleagues we've lost along the way —your spirit lives on in every airport corridor and every stretch of sky we travel. Though you are no longer with us, your stories soar in our hearts, woven into every safe journey. Your memory is cherished, and your wings are eternal.

Finally, to everyone who inspired me to write this book —you are all part of the flight plan, guiding the direction of this journey. For your faith, encouragement, and inspiration, I sincerely thank you. May our paths cross again in the sky.

With each sunrise and sunset witnessed from a window seat, and each destination welcomed with open arms, I carry profound gratitude —for the journeys behind me, the winds that lifted me, and the promise of new adventures still to come.

ABOUT THE AUTHOR

Lia spent a decade flying as a flight attendant, where her office was the cabin, and each flight created memorable stories. Her passion for human connection and appreciation for everyday beauty turned routine trips into meaningful moments.

Lia's passion for travel is boundless. She has visited all 50 states and over 70 countries and territories, aiming to see the entire world. Her dedication to exploring the beauty of our planet and making a positive impact wherever she goes remains unwavering. Her mission is to travel and inspire.

Lia divides her time between Florida and New York. When she's not writing, she's traveling, dreaming big, and inspiring others to discover wonder in the world around them.

Connect with Lia online:

	Booksbylia@gmail.com		Travel and Inspire
	AuthorLia.com		Lia Ocampo

OTHER BOOKS BY LIA OCAMPO

- What We Know for Sure: Inspirational Stories of Filipino Special Immigrants in America
- I Love Flying: An Inspirational Journal for Your Flying and Travel Adventures
- We Love Flying: How to Inspire Kids to Follow Their Dreams to Fly

www.ingramcontent.com/pod-product-compliance
Lightning Source LLC
Chambersburg PA
CBHW030409130626
46549CB00004B/1702